BY JENNY McCARTHY

Belly Laughs:
The Naked Truth About Pregnancy and Childbirth

Baby Laughs:
The Naked Truth About the First Year of Mommyhood

Life Laughs:
The Naked Truth About Motherhood,
Marriage, and Moving On

Louder than Words:
A Mother's Journey in Healing Autism

Healing and Preventing Autism:
A Complete Guide (with Dr. Jerry Kartzinel)

Mother Warriors:
A Nation of Parents Healing Autism Against All Odds

Love, Lust, & Faking It:
The Naked Truth About Sex, Lies, and True Romance

Bad Habits: Confessions of a Recovering Catholic

Jen-X: Jenny McCarthy's Open Book

Stirring the Pot:
My Recipe for Getting What You Want Out of Life

STIRRING THE POT

JENNY McCARTHY

STIRRING THE POT

My Recipe for Getting What You Want Out of Life

BALLANTINE BOOKS

NEW YORK

To the teachers who reminded me to wake up . . .
I'm awake. Thank you!

Contents

CONTENTS

STIRRING THE POT

Baby Steps

MY RECIPE FOR SUCCESS

Ingredients:

1 girl with a dream

0 financial resources

No time for bullshit

Lots of time for therapy

A heaping tablespoon of humor

2 cups of hardheadedness

Many, many disappointing setbacks

A pinch of acceptance of my place in the world

A dollop of flexibility

Directions:

Stir up ingredients and season for taste (learn to balance the sour with the sweet). Don't overmix the batter (don't overthink things; put one foot in front of the other). Simmer for life.

This'll be hard to believe given that I am now best known for being unafraid to grab a microphone and work a crowd, but when I was younger I had a totally crippling fear of public speaking. I'm not only talking about a fear of having to give a speech to the whole school or stage fright the night of the school play. That shit's *obvious*.

I was also paralyzed by something as simple as a request to read a paragraph out loud to a small class. If a teacher asked me to come to the board and show the class how to do a math problem? Hyperventilation time. Give an oral report on my science project? I'd become totally sick to my stomach and have to run to the bathroom.

To avoid getting to the puking stage, I got creative with my excuses. I conveniently "lost my glasses" a lot (even though I didn't wear any back then). I was pretty convincing with a sudden bad cough or the development of a splitting headache. One time I went so far as to quickly crack a red pen so that I could let the ink dribble down my leg. I don't know if the teacher thought my leg was bleeding or that I'd had an embarrassing female accident (as you'll see on page 61, I later became very prone to embarrassing female accidents!), but *that* was an instant pass to the nurse's office. I couldn't really use it more than once, though. Too bad.

By the time I got to college, I didn't think it was too much to hope that oral reports and front-of-class participation would be things of my past. I wanted to be a special-education major (little did I know that my son Evan's needs would give me a front-row seat in that world a decade later) and didn't see how my fear of public speaking would cause a problem. I saw myself teaching and playing with kids using blocks and games and crayons, not cue cards.

But wouldn't you know it . . . Public Speaking 101 was a requirement for my chosen major. What the fuck? There was no way around it. I knew I had to bite the bullet or I would have to give up on the thing that really interested me. I was determined. For the moment, anyway.

As I walked to class the first day, I began to shake just thinking about the *idea* of it. I can still see the big auditorium classroom now—stadium seating sloping down to a classic college lectern and about fifty shaggy students settling in to fall asleep. After introducing himself and giving an overview of the curriculum (all of which sounded terrifying and totally effing pointless to me), the professor announced that he wanted all the students to stand and briefly introduce themselves. Before even the first student had stood to tell us her name and where she was from, I had grabbed my backpack and bolted from the room.

I ran straight to the freshman guidance office and busted through the door in hysterics. I was crying so hard the advisor thought I had been attacked, and she jumped up from her chair to console me. I tried to relay the problem—my fear, the goddamned public speaking requirement—but wasn't really making much sense. When I finally managed to spit it all out, she was sympathetic to a point but also explained with a little pat on my back that most incoming freshmen were nervous about speaking in public. My response? I *really* spit it out—I put my head between my knees and vomited on the floor. Not my proudest moment. I think the counselor got the picture that my case was a little more extreme than average.

We cleaned up the puke. She calmed me down. And then we got down to business. She said she would help me find a major that didn't have a public speaking requirement. Nursing looked promising, since it was a career that would still allow me to nurture people and help people heal, and I could potentially specialize in pediatrics; I might be able to work with kids after all. I'd watched a lot of *General Hospital* and didn't think it looked so hard. Yes, I know now that was a ridiculously insane thought, and I have convinced myself all these years later that I didn't say it out loud. If I did, the counselor was cool enough to let it slide. What I do remember is that nursing didn't require me to stand up and risk shitting my pants in public. That did it for me.

I was relieved that I'd found something else that I could imagine myself doing and that wouldn't make me confront this ridiculous fear, but I also remember feeling sad and disappointed in myself because I knew that I was going to let a stupid fear keep me from a goal and a dream (special ed). A little voice in my head shamed and berated me. Not an evil-spirit mean little voice, but a wise-conscience kind of voice that told me, *You can't hide from your fear. It will find you wherever you go.*

For the most part, though, I managed to shake off the soul ache and flick the little guy off my shoulder. I kept focused on trying to pay for and not flunk out of college. For a while there I had the idea to finance my courses by selling weed. I was my own best customer, though, and spent most of my time stoned to the bone. Financially *that* wasn't working out, and educationally it wasn't so stellar, either. You try focusing on the intricacies of chemistry or biology after a wake-and-bake bender.

Not yet a nurse, and no closer to staring down my public speaking phobia, I was forced to drop out of college after my second year—no more money, no more prospects—and head back home to live with my parents. Another not-my-proudest-moment moment.

What followed were many weeks of staring at the ceiling in my old bedroom. And some sobbing. And some serious angsting about what I would do with the rest of my life. I listened to a lot of music. I ate a lot of crap food. I smoked some more weed. I sobbed some more.

And then something happened that in a movie would be depicted as the skies parting, sun shining straight down into my room, and angels singing. The camera would swing to my record collection, and out of the pile I would pull the *Grease* album with John Travolta and Olivia Newton-John looking up at me with their crazy hairdos and cheesy smiles. Inspiration had struck!

I was seven years old when I first saw *Grease*, and like so many girls at the time, I declared to my mom that I was going to go to Hollywood one day and be a star like Olivia. Of course, at seven my phobia about public speaking and performance hadn't yet taken hold—maybe my teenage hormones helped that blossom? At seven nothing stood in my way. (Just so you know, by the time I dropped out of college, I had stopped dancing around my room singing *Grease* songs into my hairbrush/microphone, but I still knew all the lyrics . . . and I still do.)

By the time I was wallowing at home and trying to figure out a new career path for myself, I was older and a little wiser and knew that making it in Hollywood would be no easy road. I'd need some connections, some auditions, some luck. Oh, and some talent. And I knew I'd need to conquer my fear of public speaking. I simply had to push through and find a way to cope with my nerves.

Whether it was Olivia's determined transformation from shy wallflower to badass leather-clad vixen (in *Grease*, that is) or the flash I had of myself drinking my sorrows away and telling anyone who would listen what I could have done with my life if only I'd had the chance (known around my house as "Irish therapy"), I was inspired to get off my ass and give acting a go.

So I opened the Yellow Pages. (For those of you who weren't around when these were in use, this is a big, yellow printed reference book with phone numbers and addresses listed alphabetically by category. Crazy, huh?) I called the Better Business Bureau and got a list of talent agencies both in my hometown, Chicago, and in Los Angeles. And then I started making calls. I begged. I pleaded. I was persistent (aka hardheaded). And as miracles or destiny would have it, I soon found myself on my way to L.A. to audition for producers.

Of course, *wanting* to conquer my fear didn't mean

I was able to. I often threw up on my way to auditions. I chewed my nails down to nubs. But I managed to hold my fears a little more in check by keeping my eyes focused on the prize: not spending my life staring at the ceiling in my childhood bedroom. I wanted this more than a degree in special education or nursing. And I was determined not to give up on a dream for a third time.

Nude modeling didn't require me to say a thing—and we all now know that I had success in that line of work. But when I did have to speak, I think I fooled people. Turns out I could *act* unafraid convincingly. And slowly, slowly the nausea turned to plain jitters and it seemed like my nerves were better under control.

Then came my very first motion picture acting job. God winked at me and saw to it that I was hired to play the part of a nurse—a nurturer and healer after all! The movie was *Things to Do in Denver When You're Dead*, and I only had one line. Drumroll, please . . . I had to say "Hello!" and then I had to feed Christopher Walken baby food for five days. I managed the hello without throwing up. Spooning food was a snap. Baby steps on the road to success.

When in Doubt, Wing It!

I t wasn't a straight shot from *Things to Do in Denver When You're Dead* to bigger and better things, but I *have* had a lot of success along the way—you bought this book presumably because you've read one or more of my other books or seen me on *The View* or in a movie (or in the nude, you perv). And unrelated to success in a dollars-and-cents sense, I've also had great happiness. In other words, I've gotten what I want out of life. So far I've gotten more than I could have hoped for, even if on the face of it there have been setbacks (my failed status as a drug lord in Carbondale, Illinois; dropping out of college; and public speaking panic attacks are just the tip of the iceberg).

If I'm being honest with myself and really trying to distill my experiences into some kind of recipe for success and happiness, I think the story of my winding path through half of college and my old-fashioned "I'm gonna make it in Hollywood" attitude is a pretty instructive first lesson. It shows that my approach to success and happiness has not exactly been calculated (wouldn't that be a boring story?). Some might say I'm naive. Or lucky. Or all those things. But that doesn't mean I can't see patterns in the messiness and can't draw some conclusions that I think might be helpful to others.

I mean, let's go back to the metaphor of a recipe for a minute. Some people follow cookbook directions precisely and want their meals to look exactly like the gourmet concoctions they see in magazines. Maybe they take classes or follow video instruction for every step. And maybe they feel pressure to get it right every time.

Me, I improvise. I might start with a written recipe, but as soon as I've figured out that I don't have all the necessary ingredients, I can confidently wing it. I open the fridge, sniff out what's gone bad, assess what might pair well with what, and then start approximating the recipe with what I *do* have on hand. The result might possibly be a gourmet meal, though it most often looks nothing like the cookbook photo. But more often than not, it looks just fine and it tastes good, too. I also know when the fridge has me beat, and I'm not too proud to call for takeout!

For as long as I can remember—from finding a way to get out of speaking in class to dealing with criticism about the way I run my mouth—I've been up on the stage of life tap-dancing my way through sticky situations with a smile on my face. I've been juggling to keep all my balls in the air (career, motherhood, and the actual male gonads in my well-documented love life). I've read my fair share of self-help books and held a mirror to myself in some questionable therapy sessions. Like anyone else, I try to learn from my mistakes (aka making the same damn bad choice over and over again until a lightbulb *finally* goes on).

I saw a public service announcement on a bus stop recently that said, "Winging it is not an emergency plan"—it was a reminder to parents to talk to their kids about what to do in the event of a disaster. I can't disagree with that in terms of disaster preparedness . . . but I don't live my life expecting the sky to fall! Winging it means being flexible, open-minded, and game for plan B if plan A doesn't pan out. There's no getting around the fact that life will be messy and imperfect and disappointing and sometimes hard. But I'm living proof that if you are open to improvisation, you can have a ton of fun and success to boot.

Try *winging it*. I highly recommend it!

Know and No

Let's agree on one thing: whatever method there is to my madness, I am *not* someone who has made success look easy. My path to success has been long and winding. Actually, it's been more like a roller coaster—more ups and downs than lefts and rights. But trial and error, as well as setbacks and kicks in the teeth, make you appreciate whatever measure of success you ultimately enjoy. No ache, no appreciation, that's what I say.

And let's be honest: I've stepped in more shit than I could ever begin to scrape off my shoes. At least the reason for *that* is clear. Except possibly for *not* sharing my "watching *General Hospital* means I could be a nurse" theory, I have made a habit of not considering the consequences of whatever I'm about to say before I say it.

I like to think that speaking my mind is part of my charm, but that's just an after-the-fact rationalization. I don't say what's on my mind to be charming. Obviously not, because I don't just put my foot in my mouth; I often swallow it whole. I don't care how easy some exotic dancers make that look; it's not an especially comfortable position to be in.

Another way to say it? No one has ever accused me of being a closed book. Instead, my friends have been known to say, "Puleeeeeaze put a cork in it!" What I *think* is what you get. (Except for my rack, what you see is what you get, too. My rack has been surgically altered a couple of times—I can't lie.)

Given all that, and given the fact that you expected some advice when you bought this book, let me mouth off a little for you here. Allow me to break my theory of happiness down for you a little further. Based on my highly scientific study of the phenomenon (aka my own life), I can tell you that there are several things we all need to *know* and also a couple of necessary *no*s to learn about for good measure.

Know Yourself

Knowing yourself in some big, psychological sense means you are in touch with your feelings and your motivations, and if you're truly evolved (that is, no longer blaming Mom and Dad for everything), you have accepted your shortcomings as your own.

But there's another way to know yourself that's more mundane but not less important: you know what you can tolerate and what you just can't. When you know yourself in this way, you don't waste time pretending you're someone you're not, and you can voice your discomfort instead of pretending you're the happiest lady on the block. (See "Decade-by-Decade Decision Making," page 27, for more on this profound topic!)

An example: me, I'm not outdoorsy, and I just can't pretend that I am. Angelina Jolie's regular trips to Africa are inspiring, but I'll just have to write her a check to support her cause. For me, going to Italy is roughing it! I know they've got nice accommodations all over Italy, but I also know that I need a Vegas-style, big-ass bathroom, or I'm nothing to nobody. If you see a photo of me barefoot by a fire pit in Zimbabwe, you know that either it's a fake set or some producer threatened to fire me if I didn't make that trek and have that photo taken. Know this: I may be smiling, but I'm not happy or comfortable sitting at that fire pit. Of course, grinning and bearing it is something we all have to do from time to time, but grinning and trying to convince yourself you're happy is a waste of time. You're welcome—I just saved you years of therapy.

A less trivial example: I knew when to stop having babies.

I love and need my kid like air. He's a total blessing and I cannot, cannot, cannot imagine my life without him. But I don't need the kid in my life to become plural. Kids take time and focus, and I know myself enough to know my limit is to focus on just one. Having one child allows me to say yes to his needs *and* to have a work life, too. I wasn't cut out to be the mother of five who has no time for herself. No apologies there, people. I know my limits and my limitations!

Be Able to Say "I Don't F*cking Know"

I've always had trouble sleeping. Wait, let me take that back. I've had trouble sleeping since I was old enough to start worrying about jobs, bills, and boys. I often lie in bed and contemplate and ruminate and waste my precious sleeping hours. It's exhausting. Vodka, NyQuil, or Ambien can be helpful (never all three!), but it's been clear for a while that I need to find another way of shutting off my mind.

Well, a solution recently hit me square in the face. In an offhanded way—totally casual and not at all preachy—a wise friend of mine recently said, "Don't ask yourself questions you can't possibly know the answers to." I'm sure we were shopping at the time and I was asking why the seams on my jeans were a different color than the seams on the ones she was wearing. Or maybe I had just peeled a callus off my foot and asked why it was shaped like the state of Illinois.

But wow. Even if we weren't talking about deep spiritual enlightenment at the time, that was an Oprah lightbulb moment for me. "Don't ask yourself questions you can't possibly know the answers to." Fucking mind-blowing, that's what it is. I couldn't think of a more brilliant statement or one that would better help me shut down the "what if?" and "will I?" questions that keep me up at night.

LETTING GO OF KNOWING: A RECIPE FOR SUCCESS

Need another strategy for holding worry at bay? This works for me. Whether the concern is about my job, a guy, or the amount of my next royalty check, I try to imagine it as a bar of soap I'm holding in my hand in the shower. If I squeeze the soap tight to try to control it, it slips out of my hand. So the next time you are consumed with worry or obsessed with making something happen, *stop squeezing the soap.*

Know How to Say No

We all know someone in our lives who overuses their favor card. It doesn't matter if they overstep just one time too many or ten—one favor too many is too many. (If this describes you, you seriously need to stop this shit before you don't have any friends left.)

Sure, it's great to help out a friend in need, but when the favors outnumber the quality time spent, you're probably being used. Is there someone in your life you call only when you need something, or are you on the other end of that phone call rolling your eyes at a friend who didn't call to talk but instead called to ask for something (a "tiny" favor, a loan) again? Ever heard of the *power of a loving no*? Get comfortable with it. A huge part of self-love is being able to stand up for yourself when you are feeling taken advantage of.

Be Able to Take No for an Answer

Sometimes people say no because what you've asked is unreasonable in the first place: "No, I can't find you a five-star hotel with a Vegas-style bathroom near the set in Zimbabwe."

Sometimes people say no because even though they would like to help you, they honestly can't: "No, Jenny, I'm sorry, but my hands are tied. You and your sister got yourselves axed from Madonna's after-Oscars party this year because of the Thailand-style strip club performance you gave there last year."

Sometimes people say no because they are law-abiding wimps: "No, we can't keep the bar open for you and your friends. We will lose our liquor license."

And sometimes people say no because they are ass-holes and it makes them feel temporarily good about themselves to insult you while they are denying your request: "No, you can't star opposite Brad Pitt because you are past your prime."

The High Road?

Wait, wait, wait . . . did you interpret that last chapter to mean that I think you should always turn the other cheek? Ha! Being able to take no for an answer doesn't always mean that you have to take someone else's shit. Repeat after me: when it comes to gracefully reacting to an obvious or implied criticism, you *do not* always have to take the high road. In fact, I urge you to develop your sense of where the shorter, more direct route lies and when taking it just might be the best course of action.

Let's work on that. See if you can spot the correct response to each of the following situations from my own life.

Scenario 1: Evan has just swatted my hand away from his dinner plate while making a heinous seagull caw-cawing noise as he flaps his arms like wings. In other words, he has just cleverly accused me of being a food scavenger. (Yes, this happens all the time.)

Should I (A) flip his plate over on the floor to express my disgust and then mock his seagull noise by making the snorting sound of a pig, or (B) give him a high five and then silently take a bow for having raised a young man who's both observant and funny?

That one was easy. (Wait, you said A, right? No need to take crap from an eleven-year-old and/or take the high road in the comfort of your own home.)

Scenario 2: I'm walking into the lobby of my apartment building after a long day of work and a "reporter" (you get quote marks if you're from TMZ, guys) appears out of nowhere, shoves a microphone in my face, and yells (it always feels like they're yelling!), "Hey, Jenny, why is it that you can't seem to stay in a relationship?" Or maybe he shouts, "Hey, Jenny, is it true you're about to be fired?"

Should I (A) give him the benefit of the doubt and choose to hear his question as a compliment? You know, choose to hear "You help our ratings when we can flash a photo of you out on a date with someone new, so thanks and keep up the speed dating!" or "A nasty and public fight over your day job would sure sell magazines, so we're rooting for you to get canned ASAP!" Or should I (B) make a heinous seagull caw-cawing noise at him (to express my feeling that he is scavenging off the crumbs of my life) and colorfully tell him where he can shove it?

Right again! "Reporters" always deserve the benefit of the doubt.

Scenario 3: On the rare occasion I happen to be listening to National Public Radio (let's assume that I'm trapped in a town car and I'm too polite to ask the driver to change to dance tunes), I overhear someone being interviewed about special-needs parenting. The highly educated expert interviewee says confidently, "Jenny McCarthy doesn't know what she's talking about."

Should I (A) whip out my cell phone and call the radio show so that I can give the "world-class researcher" (also often deserving of quote marks) a swear-laden monologue about my half semester as a special-ed major, for one thing, and oh, gee, maybe explain the difference between laboratory statistics and what a mother sees with her own eyes? Or should I (B) bemusedly place the criticism in context while calmly reminding myself that debate is good and that none of us has all the answers, then ask the driver to change to dance tunes after all?

I'm not going to tell you the right answer to that one. I know you'll choose wisely.

Decade-by-Decade
Decision Making

'm in my four tens now. My very early four tens, but
I'm in them fair and square.

Four tens: that's the way to say forties using the
Singapore Math method that they're teaching kids
these days. I didn't appreciate the merits of Singapore
Math at first, but then I figured out that it's a handy
way of confusing people about how old you are, how
much you weigh, or how much money you make (if
they are totally rude enough to ask any of those questions). The only people who are going to immediately
know what you're talking about are the good citizens
of Singapore and the small American children who are
using it now to learn to count. Neither of those popu-
lations gives a crap what the answers to any of those
questions are. Win-win.

When I was in my two tens (when you actually
mostly want people to think you're older than you are,
the whole Singapore Math confusion doesn't help the
cause), I was very adventurous. You could convince me

to eat chocolate-covered scorpions or jump out of a plane, and I would try any diet or exercise fad if it had a celebrity endorsement. I'd drive to Vegas on a whim or take off on a trip to who knows where with who knows whom at the drop of a hat. In your twenties you're still trying to catalogue the things that turn you on. You're on a fact-finding mission to experience the things that will become reference points for your future taste. In the process you learn which things you never want to try again. Discovery—good and bad—is a thrill in its own right.

In my three tens (stay with me here, math morons— that means my thirties), I was still pretty open to trying new things. The experience of motherhood was one of those things, as were germy indoor ball pits (nightmares), Mommy and Me classes (snore), and strained peaches (so damn delicious).

Probably because of becoming a mother, the three tens were also a time when I began to develop a better alarm system for *when* to try new things. I learned that there is a time for cutting loose and a time to take a pass in favor of going with what you know you like and what you need.

Take restaurants. In my three tens I had a couple of favorite "no reason except that it's Thursday" restaurants and only tried a new place or a new dish if it was a "special occasion." Not that Thursday isn't special in its very own way, but on Thursdays it was usually just my son, Evan, and me, and I didn't want surprises. That still holds true. When I'm on the mommy clock, I want predictable routine with the highest chance of happiness for our time together. A Thursday place is where I go to get the food that I know Evan likes, and the grilled cheese and tomato soup I know they make so well. Veal scaloppini? Thank you for the offer, it sounds delicious, but I want the thing that I *know* makes me happy and that I might be able to share with my son.

And so here I am in my four tens and I am happy to be able to say that I have a pretty finely tuned sense of what I like and what I don't like. More important, I have a good sense for what might be worth trying (hey, I'm still pretty game!) and what I can't be talked into trying or liking on the grounds that it's on someone else's bucket list. For instance, I don't have to go to jail to know I wouldn't like it. (There was a time in my two tens when even *that* experience sounded like it might be worth having, if only to have a story to tell.)

At four tens I'm a pretty good judge of what is worth my time and what I can go without trying in favor of honoring what I know to be true for me. That doesn't mean that I've completely sworn off trying new things, just that I'm old enough to know that I'm not going to miss out by not trying everything that comes my way.

As Popeye said before popping a can of spinach into his piehole: "I yam what I yam." And man, it feels good to have arrived at this stage of the game.

Try Anything Once

```
RECIPE FOR SUCCESS
■ ■ ■ ■ ■ ■ ■ ■ ■ ■ ■ ■ ■ ■ ■ ■ ■ ■

Ingredients:
  An open mind
  The ability to laugh at yourself
  The ability to not laugh out loud at someone else's
    expense
  A little upper-body strength (optional)
```

In the game of Truth or Dare, I've always been one to pick the dare. Telling the truth just isn't much of a challenge for me. As you know, I'm only too happy to tell you what's on my mind and to admit to what I've done.

I'm also a sucker for pretty much any self-help book or self-improvement program out there. Which means either that I need a lot of help or that I'm an evolved soul always searching for a new level of consciousness. Care to take a stab at which?

But what happens when you put my interest in challenge and self-improvement together?

Well, take color therapy. Totally mind-blowing, that one. Better (healthier and more relaxing, certainly) than a good ride on Ecstasy.

During my first color therapy session, the guru/goddess/high-priestess/practitioner/licensed-by-some-entity/woman-in-charge talked a lot about the meaning of various colors and explained all about portals and openings and being open to letting things flow in. Ya, I had to hold back a laugh, too, but get your mind out of the gutter . . . she was talking about spiritual passageways! Then she placed a bunch of colored bottles in front of me and asked me to choose those that "spoke" to me. I listened hard, but none spoke up clearly. The green one seemed to be clearing her throat to say something but never got much further than that. In the end, I just picked the colors I thought were pretty, green among them.

Next, she had me lie down on a massage table and sprayed mist in my chosen colors around me while tinkly music played in the background. Then she placed the colored bottles at key chakras on my body. She balanced one on my forehead, placed one at my feet, and put three at my crotch. Should I have questioned the focus on my crotch? I didn't. I just giggled.

After an hour and a half of listening to the trippy music and lying still so as not to disturb the bottles, I actually felt floaty and started seeing colors, too. Oddly, this was *way* better than a deep muscle massage. The stillness was kind of a revelation. (Or maybe there was something funky in the colorful mist I had inhaled?)

As much as I wanted to laugh at the whole idea at the start, I have to admit that I now see colors as being deeply meaningful. Turquoise, for instance, is apparently a color that helps you express your thoughts through the heart. Hey, maybe I'd talk less out my ass if I wore it more often. I'll try it. That said, turquoise also happens to be a color that indicates a connection to dolphins and to the lost city of Atlantis. I can't find a way to make those things relevant in my life (and wardrobe people are great, but they really don't care about these things), so I just focus on the talking-through-the heart benefit.

Another wacky "therapy"? Tapping. Not Gene Kelly tapping with shoes. Tapping with fingers. Your own. As self-administered therapy. It's called the Emotional Freedom Technique (EFT), and the theory is that tapping on certain pressure points—your wrists, your chest, you name it—will help you resolve issues and attain goals. I have to admit that I found the tap-

tap-tapping soothing. I can also admit that having to focus on a specific body part while thinking about a specific problem has a way of focusing the issue. It's not something you want to do in public, though, because you end up looking like you have multiple personality disorder and one of your personalities is Woody Woodpecker. I'd also rather have someone *else* tap on a certain body part while I focus on pleasure for a while, if you know what I mean.

And then there's rock climbing, a challenge I put myself through recently that was decidedly less relaxing. I'm not sure why I thought this kind of outdoorsy, roughing-it thing would be any more enjoyable than, say, that fire pit in Zimbabwe, but I'd heard you can get a rush from the danger, so I gave it a try. I do not recommend it. No high, just PTSD.

Even without the snow-covered rock face and terrible weather conditions like you see in a North Face ad (because this was an indoor facility), and even wearing a harness that had been tightened, checked, and rechecked, I could only get myself to the first level of the climbing structure—about ten feet off the ground. Rock climbing takes upper-body strength, but more than anything, it takes *balls*. I thought I had them. Apparently not enough. I couldn't force myself to climb any higher and told the instructor she was just going to have to build me a little platform and hoist my meals up in a basket. With lots of coaxing (something tells me that my kind of paralysis was not new to them), the instructor talked me into letting go of the support beam I was clinging to and allowing her to lower me down via the ropes and harness. I will say that *that* part of the program was cool—I liked the feeling of briefly floating in space. There are simpler ways of getting that kind of high, though. And it's now legal in several states.

Last but not least (and no doubt not last, either), there's my attempt at the twenty-one-day Complaint Free challenge. A self-help guru named Will Bowen thought this one up, arguing that complaining is manipulative, reveals low self-worth, is physically and psychologically unhealthy, alienates friends and family, is addictive, and stops us from realizing our dreams. Seems like kind of an overreaction to a mostly harmless little complaint, don't you think? I would argue that as addictions go, complaining is pretty G-rated. Complaining doesn't cause tooth decay, liver disease, or bankruptcy. Just saying.

But I'm game and open-minded, remember?

The basic idea is that you wear a rubber bracelet—like the Lance Armstrong one, but in purple—and switch it to your other wrist every time you complain (only spoken complaints count; you are allowed to complain in your mind as much as you want). The goal is to go twenty-one consecutive days without switching the bracelet at all. Anytime you have to switch the bracelet to your other wrist, the clock goes back to day one and you start again. Apparently, when you finish—um, *if* you finish, or if you *claim* to have finished—you can go to Bowen's website and order a "Certificate of Happiness." Not to complain or anything, but that sounds to me more like something you get after completing a course in tantric sex.

Within just a couple of days of starting (and restarting) the challenge, I discovered three things:

1. Complaining bonds people. The magic of several of my closest friendships is that we can comfortably and safely bitch about others to each other. Much as I'd like to finish what I started, I realized that I don't want to give that pressure valve up just yet.

2. The bracelet kind of worked like the tapping I described above: it focused me on the fact that I tend to complain mindlessly. So I started to complain more deliberately. I feel better already.

3. A Certificate of Happiness is something I can award myself!

In the end, it's hard for me to say that I truly regret any challenge or therapy I've done in the name of self-improvement. Wait—actually, see page 76 for my feelings about juice detoxing, and if I were you, I'd not eat Chiclets off someone's ass. There was actually a self-help angle involved in that episode (none of your business), but you cannot remove that kind of imagery from your mental hard drive no matter how much tapping you do.

THE WHINE-FREE SPRITZER

Another way to quit whining? Ditch the wine and stick with the hard stuff:

Ingredients:

3 ounces (decent) bourbon

2 ice cubes

1 ounce soda water

Girls' Night In

If I were to make a list of the great loves of my life,
several on the list would be women. No, I'm not coming out in these pages! I'm simply saying that some of
my female friends have loved me more and known me
better than some of the men I've palled around with.

For all the excitement and intimacy that goes along

with a romantic relationship, sexual attraction can cloud your judgment, and sexual tension can build resentment (not to mention resentments over dirty laundry, left-up toilet seats, and the other annoyances of cohabitation). With family members, for better or for worse, there's baggage. But with certain girlfriends, you can take off the mask you wear during the day— wife, girlfriend, daughter, mother, colleague, Girl Scout, or bitch—and just be you, which may be a little of all those things, but not just one. Girlfriends are happily leaned on. Which reminds me that all the talk about leaning *in* to our careers and our goals in life somehow misses a big part of the point: leaning *on* each other is the way to get ahead! Best girlfriends pick each other up when they're down, celebrate each other's successes, and coach self-forgiveness after major fuck-ups.

Given that outpouring of mushy girl-adoration, it'll come as no surprise to you that girls' night is a date I hold sacred on my calendar.

In my two tens (see page 27 for an explanation), girls' night meant girls' night *out on the town*. Short dresses, high heels, candy-colored cocktails with fruit skewers or umbrellas. Good tunes, good times. We'd get dolled up, go dancing, and protect each other as we explored the hell out of the world.

Even if the club we went to was dead and no one bought us drinks or the guy we liked wanted someone else's number, it didn't matter because we were together. We were invincible! Put together, the three or four of us were a six- or eight-legged, glossy-lipped, sexy beast. Girl power! (So the next time you see a pack of young girls out on the town like that, resist the urge to think that their tipsiness or their seeming availability means that they are shallow and careless. Trust me, they are less on the prowl for men than they are on the prowl for adventure. They are celebrating their freedom, their femininity, and the safety they feel when together. End of lecture!)

Now that I'm older-ish, girls' night *in* is the thing for me. Being dressed to the nines in a trendy nightclub has its merits and I still go that route from time to time, but I'm less into the pounding dance beats, laser lights, and the jackasses who try to take a selfie on their smartphone with me.

Now when I get together with my girlfriends I want to wear sweats or pajamas, eat good food, drink really good wine, and indulge in great conversation. And then I want to ice the cake by binge-watching an entire season of a television show featuring handsome, chivalrous, or devious Englishmen, or the vicarious drunkenness of the movie *Bridesmaids*. The concept is still the same—we are celebrating our freedom (because Lord knows it gets harder and harder to coordinate as we all get busier with kids and careers), our femininity, and the safety we feel in each other's company.

How many more ways can I say it?

Hands down, girls' night *in* body-slams almost anything else in the cage match of fun.

Girls' night *in* is a staycation from my daily troubles. It's more rejuvenating than a trip to the day spa and more nourishing than ninety minutes of hot yoga.

I look forward to girls' night *in* more than Black Friday sales or Chris Hemsworth films.

It's Christmas without all the shitty seasonal coffee creamer flavors and pressure. (A side note to the person who approved the creation of eggnog latte creamer: if you won't quit, you're fired!)

DISGUISED PIZZA (AKA PEAR GORGONZOLA FLATBREAD)

■ ■

Ingredients:

1 ball of store-bought pizza dough (per guest if you're not dieting!)

1 pear

A handful of Gorgonzola cheese

A handful of arugula

½ lemon

1 tablespoon olive oil

Salt and pepper

Directions:

Preheat the oven to 450 degrees.

Using a little flour so that your hands don't stick to the dough, stretch the pizza dough into a flatbread shape and place it on a sheet pan or pizza stone. Thinly slice a pear, then line pear slices up on the dough all pretty-like. Sprinkle Gorgonzola cheese over pear slices. Bake in the oven for 10–15 minutes. While that is baking, clean the arugula and squeeze lemon juice over the greens. Add olive oil, salt, and pepper. Toss. The flatbread is done when the cheese is melty, the pears tender, and the crust golden. Top the hot pizza—whoops, flatbread—with arugula.

Five Things You Don't Want to Hear at a Class Reunion

1. Weren't you a dude?

2. Weren't you voted Most Likely to Succeed? What happened?

3. What class did you teach?

4. So what time do you have to report back to your parole officer?

5. I was sad when you broke up with me, but I eventually got over it. Listen, my helicopter is here, so I need to go. Good luck with your door-to-door costume jewelry business. I'll check you out on Pinterest!

Drunk and Disorderly in the Age of Social Media

Texting or tweeting is hard enough when you're sober. First there are those tiny little buttons on your phone. And in my case, big old clumsy thumbs. Recipe for disaster right there. Add the fact that I'm usually in a cab or walking down the street or trying to pretend I'm listening to you while trying to type, and you get some crazy-ass messages.

Add alcohol to the equation? Well, if you think I'm uninhibited when I'm sober, you ain't seen the half of it.

When I'm drinking with friends, they usually help keep my thumb diarrhea in check. Text policing is just another thing that good friends do for each other, after all. Where I run into trouble is after they've dropped me off or when they've all gone home (or when I'm drinking alone). Some recent examples of my late-night outreach to the friends I have been drinking with:

"CAN U COME OVER AND BRUSH MY TEETH?"

"OH NO. Cunt find batteries for vibrator. Do u have AAs? Cum quick."

Or this beauty that I sent to my agent:

"Thoughts on expanding career. Go with me. What about playing Meryl Streep's daughter who decides to end her life, but its funny? If not Streep, maybe Cher? Make a note to look up A-listers who can play mom to me. never mind, I just made the note myself and stuck it to the phone so I wont forget. But, seriously, lets keep thinking outside the box. Because my box isn't getting younger. Hah!!!"

Or this one to Evan's teacher:

Dear Ms. West,
I luv you so much. Don't be afraid to talk to me outside of class.
You can call me Jenny. Or anytime.
Kisses,
Jenny

Or this to a local dog shelter:

Dear dog people,
Please stop sending pictures of sad-looking dogs. It
makes me so sad and even though they are cute and
sad I can't take another dog, because you know how
it is. So stop. Please stop it because I am crying
now.
Jenny

Or this email to myself:

Subject: DON'T FORGET: READ THIS WHEN
YOU WAKE UP. Go get the morning-after pill.
Love, me

Seven Things I Wish
Someone Would Invent

1. An app that can detect your blood alcohol level through the keys on your phone. When you're texting late at night (see previous chapter) it will block your message and politely ask in a computerized voice, "Is sending this [angry rant/indecent proposal/picture of your ass] the strongest choice you can make right now?"

2. On a related note, how about a device that allows you to erase any message you have sent—text, email, or voicemail—if it hasn't been viewed or listened to yet? Sure would cut down on my drunk dialing. Wait, has that already been invented? Somebody send me a message!

3. Did you ever see that Michael Douglas movie *The Game*? Someone hires a company to trick Michael Douglas's character into thinking his life is in danger and that he's gotten mixed up in a dark,

dangerous world. The hoax is amazingly elaborate, and it's done to make MD reconsider what a dick he's been all his life. Well, I'd like to hire a company like that, a whole team of actors and stuntmen and hundreds of people in on the scheme—but I wouldn't use the service to mess with people like in that movie. Instead, I'd hire them when I needed breakup help. I don't mind being made the bad guy—just find a way to make the person I want to ditch think it's all my fault and not his so that he'll walk and I won't have to!

4. I know stolen cars can be recovered through Lo-Jack, and pets can get a microchip so owners can locate them when they get lost. I heard somewhere they make them for kids now, too. But how about a tracking chip that could be inserted in your boyfriend or husband without him knowing? A little something I could stuff into the olive of his next martini? Or put in his toothpaste? Or slip painlessly up his nose while he's sleeping?

5. While I'm wishing and hoping, how about something that makes anything from *Star Trek* possible . . . like a beaming-up device that would allow me to skip my commute, or at least a warp-speed attachment for my car?

6. The world also needs a roofie detector. They should be built into cocktail straws and put in every bar. If someone slips a roofie into your drink, the little wand thing would immediately send a text to the bartender so he or she could be sure you don't leave the premises, and it would also send an emergency message to the nearest police department. Take that, pervy strangers!

7. Last but not least, is it too much to ask for someone to invent no-hangover alcohol pills? I hate having to make such an effort to get my buzz on (all that sipping is *such* hard work). I want to swallow four vodka or tequila pills and then avoid the frying-pan-to-the-forehead feeling the next day. I know there are pills already available that would do the trick, but I want my no-hangover alcohol pills to be totally legal and FDA regulated (because the FDA *always* knows what's best). Oh, and these pills should be zero-calorie and made from all-natural ingredients. I'll buy stock in your company if you're working on this.

Poke Me

It's news to no one that there are millions of ways to waste your time online, right? One minute you're looking for a clever synonym for "useless" on thesaurus .com, and click, click, click . . . suddenly three hours have gone by and you've lived the word in any number of ways: you've watched nine previews for movies that won't be in theaters for another six months, you've taken a quiz to see if your boyfriend might really be a narcissist, you've looked at the red carpet snapshots of the best- and worst-dressed at the Oscars going back three years, you've read an obscure article about the Estonian synchronized swimming team, you've tweeted about how inspiring those Estonians really are, you've checked flight costs to Rio in the event you decide to cheer on the Estonians in 2016, and you've connected with three new people on Facebook that you think you knew in preschool.

And if you're like me, you did all that when you could have and should have been playing outside with your son.

I've tried to curb my surfing/email/Facebook/Twitter/Pinterest addiction, really I have. I *know* that I should give my son my undivided attention and never miss a moment of his childhood. I've read all the books, too, and I've beat myself up plenty. But here's the thing that I know a lot of moms will agree with. I'm going to go out on a limb and say that sometimes little kids are boring. Sometimes their stories reveal their creative and emotional development, but . . . sometimes the story is really just about a Play-Doh snake. And sometimes, given the choice, even the most inane online crap is more stimulating than conversation with them.

For example, texting with a friend about what might happen on the next episode of *Downton Abbey* engages my brain to think about European history (what real-life event *will* they tackle next?) and the nuances of television character development. Talking about the last *SpongeBob* episode . . . not so much.

Looking at photos of my friend's crazy night out in Vegas is nothing if not entertaining. Hearing stories about the kite at school that was painted red . . . not so much.

Taking online tours of five-star vacation villas? Okay, I'll admit that this is a slight waste of time, because building a pillow fort in the living room will be another fun way to think about real estate. But seriously, don't deny me this little pleasure. Isn't there a way I can do both in the same afternoon?

Of course, the irony is that just about the only thing that can get me to stop surfing, chatting, posting, or Skyping and pay attention to other humans is some good old-fashioned human connection. I need a real, live poke.

And the truly ironic thing is that the best poker in the world is the kid I am studiously ignoring with my online addictions. It's true, and he now knows it: if Evan crawls up on my lap or tugs on my sleeve and wants to snuggle, I'm putty in his hands pretty much instantly. If he bats his eyelashes on my cheek like a butterfly, rubs my nose like an Eskimo, or gives me a traditional peck, I'm all his. Let's go build that fort in the living room and roll some Play-Doh snakes. My 4G connection can wait!

The Red Scare

D
o all McCarthys get the same lame jokes made at their expense at cocktail parties or is it just me? When I am introduced to people of a certain age (as in anyone older than me), it almost never fails that they chuckle about the possibility of me being related to Joseph McCarthy, the Communist-hating American senator who died in 1957. As though old Joe and I are the only Irish American Catholic dropouts (him from junior high, temporarily, and me from college, permanently) on the planet?

To all those aging jokesters and to anyone my age or younger who knows or cares what Joseph McCarthy did with his time on earth, I'd like to try to wash his image from your mind and replace his brand of McCarthyism with my own. To start, let me try to change what you see and hear when someone says "the Red Scare." Male reader discretion advised . . .

Like most teenage girls, I found my mother endlessly embarrassing. I'm not too proud to admit now that she was mostly doing nothing wrong and really didn't deserve my eye rolling and bitchy attitude. But there was one area of her life that she found embarrassing, too; neither of us could get over the mortification! It was this: she couldn't get a handle on her periods. On several occasions I had to go into the house to get her a towel so she could get out of the car without scaring the neighborhood.

She once even had a bleed-out in church! She held our family back from filing out of the pews until everyone else had left the building, and then she dashed out the side door with someone's sweater tied around her waist. Afterward, I tried to keep track of her periods, not so that I could be helpful to her but so that I could plan to stay the hell away from her at that time of the month! Couldn't she just wear a frigging diaper when she had her period?

"Just wait until you've had kids and this happens to you," she said wisely (and patiently and kindly—my mom really is the greatest). I wasn't having any of it—I was a very careful period planner and knew that I would always have a good handle on them and always be prepared. I was sure that I was *not* going to be anything like my mother in that regard.

Of course, the apple (smashed cherry, perhaps?) never falls far from the tree, does it? My gynecologist tells me it doesn't happen to everyone, but clearly we McCarthy women are doubly cursed. It's not that I lose track of when I'm getting them or that they are irregular (yet), but my periods became Carrie-at-the-prom heavy after I had Evan. (Google that movie and watch the blood drip down the walls!) I wish a red blotch on my skirt at church was the worst of my accidents.

To date, here are a few examples of my syndrome in action:

Onstage

During its Charlie Sheen years, I guest-starred on *Two and a Half Men*. I had several scenes with Charlie. No winging it allowed—I had to be funny and zany and sexy but all on cue, and I had to do it in front of a live studio audience. But on the day in question, my dam broke mid-scene.

I had thought ahead, I swear I had. I was plugged up good with tampons, plus I was wearing a nighttime-strength maxi pad. But nothing ever happens quickly or totally on schedule when you're shooting for TV (or movies), and I'd just been up on that stage too long. I knew when my defenses had been breached. If anything like this has happened to you, you know the feeling. You know you've started to color outside the lines. You know you have to get to the bathroom to refortify, but you also know that any movement to get *to* the bathroom could be disastrous.

Until the take was over, my only option was to cross my legs and clench as hard as I could. And though I should have been focusing on my next line, I couldn't concentrate on anything but what my excuse would be if blood spattered on the floor. I figured I could try to blame it on Charlie and claim he must have had a bloody nose. Given his lifestyle at the time, it was conceivable that people would believe me (Charlie himself might even have been easily fooled).

Fortunately, I didn't have to lie about Charlie's drug-weakened nasal passages—the director said "cut" and I asked for a five-minute break to use the facilities.

I obviously needed to get off the stage quickly, but I couldn't take big steps and I couldn't risk letting the studio audience see my ass; I had no idea what kind of red splotch would be blooming there. My only option was to shuffle offstage while continuing to face forward. Kind of like the characters on *South Park*. Shuffle, shuffle, shuffle stage left, and I was out of there.

Once I was safely in the bathroom I could assess the damage. As I'd thought, I was a mess. There was no going back out there with the same pants on—they would need to be tossed. I stuck my head out the bathroom door and called for reinforcements: "Hello? Any female on the set, please, any female?" A young woman from the wardrobe department materialized, and I let her in. She went white when she saw the carnage. Sweet, naive, pre-motherhood girl that she was, she asked me if I'd just had a miscarriage.

Forgive me, Father, for I have sinned . . . I *seriously* considered lying and telling her that she'd found me out. The sympathy would have been helpful at that point. But for once I wasn't quick enough on my feet. I couldn't tell that lie. I had to admit that I was just a gusher and couldn't control my body for more than about twenty- or thirty-minute increments at this time of the month. I imagined she was making a mental note to never get older as she left to search for a replacement pair of pants.

A few minutes later I was ready to go: I had the whole feminine products aisle tucked right where it all should go—a super-duper-duper tampon and, this time, two pads. I walked bowlegged back to the set and got on with the work of the day, asking for "pee breaks" as often as I could.

The Mile-High Club

Okay, I told a white lie about never being surprised by my period. Sometimes I'm blindsided just like everyone else.

Recently I was blindsided while buckled groggily into seat 3A of an American Airlines flight. I was heading back home after being in a different time zone (which I'm going to blame for my miscalculation about what day it was). We had to wait on the runway for two hours—two hours of not getting up and moving around the cabin, and two hours of increasingly odd and uncomfortable cramping.

By the time we were cleared for takeoff and the seat belt sign was off, I was pretty sure I was in trouble *down there*. I got up as fast as I could and crammed myself into one of those outrageously small and oddly lit coffins they call restrooms. I'd had the presence of mind to bring my purse with me, but my heart sank when I realized that all my emergency absorbent supplies were packed away in the bag that I'd checked. What the fuck is wrong with me? An emergency stash like that must be kept on you at all times! I know, I know.

Of course I wasn't the first nor will I be the last woman forced to do the only thing there is to do in that desperate and disgusting situation: I made a homemade maxi pad by wrapping half a roll of toilet paper around my hand and shoving the "pad" into place in my underwear.

Now, if multiple tampons and maxi pads don't even work for me on these heavy flow days, I don't know why I ever thought that half a roll of one-ply would do the trick. (And is it even one-ply? Tracing paper would be a better description!) But what choice did I really have? I would just have to return to the bathroom every twenty to thirty minutes and keep spinning out my homemades. I washed my hands and returned to my seat to bleed—I mean sweat—it out.

Over the course of the long flight I managed to stem the tide of the Red Sea by keeping myself awake and re-creating the pad at regular intervals. When we neared our destination, however, the captain asked us to stay in our seats for the remaining forty minutes of our descent. I didn't panic. I just focused on not sneezing, coughing, or breathing until we'd touched down and I could visit the bathroom one more time before heading out to get my luggage.

Forty minutes passed, then forty-five, then fifty. I needed to get up. I needed to get fresh TP. But we were nowhere near touchdown! The captain came back on and said something like, "As you've probably noticed, we have been circling due to weather and it doesn't look like we're going to be able to land anytime soon. So we are going to change course and land at the nearest airfield to refuel. We'll attend to all of this as quickly as possible and get back in the air and back on our way as soon as possible. I'll keep you updated on our progress." All I really heard was, "You're screwed."

Did you happen to see the look on Will and Jada Pinkett Smith's faces during Miley Cyrus's twerking performance at the Video Music Awards? They were right there in the front row and were clearly more than a little horrified. That's more or less the face I made.

I caught the eye of one of the flight attendants, who was safely buckled into her own rear-facing seat a couple of feet from me. I pointed at my crotch and mouthed, "I'm bleeding and I don't have anything!"

The look on her face told me that she felt my pain. The look on the other flight attendant's face was a little less understanding. Embarrassed is more like it. *He* looked kind of in shock and then down at his hands. His female counterpart whispered that I should just go into the bathroom anyway and stay there while she hunted around for a tampon. That's the power of the sisterhood right there!

After a few minutes, my newfound friend and fairy godmother knocked on the door. Sitting on the toilet seat, I opened the door enough for her to both hand me a tampon and see the *Nightmare on Elm Street* damage to my undercarriage. I had bled through the jeans that were now around my ankles, and there was no disguising it. Her eyes widened, but— diplomatically, expertly, and helpfully—she held up a finger as if to say "Just a minute" and disappeared back around the door. I heard some whispering, and then a few moments later she knocked again and handed me the male flight attendant's jacket! "He said you can keep it. He's a fan."

My hero and savior had unbuckled and made himself scarce by the time I came out of the bathroom, and he and I didn't make eye contact again for the rest of the flight. But when I was leaving the plane at long last, he was the one at the door wishing passengers a good day and thanking us all for our patience. I wanted to kiss his sweet face and thank him for his kindness but instead just patted the jacket that was now tied around my waist and whispered that *I* was *his* biggest fan.

A Classy Charity Event

I am not a golfer, but I'll do anything to raise money for a good cause, even if the businessmen and politicians who have paid $10,000 to take that nice walk on the pretty green grass with you really just want to see you bend over in your Daisy Dukes. When you're wearing short-shorts and you have your period, however, some of those big spenders probably want their money back. Especially when you steal their golf cart on the third tee in order to get your uterus back to the safety of the clubhouse locker room and you never come back to the links. Sorry, fellas!

After each of these Red Scares I have called my mother to commiserate, to apologize for my insensitivity when she was going through this physical passage, and to let her laugh at me until she cries. She tells me that there are still more surprises to come in terms of the way I might experience menopause. I know some women don't enjoy going through that particular "change of life" and others think we only get sexier with age (Suzanne Somers, I'm talking to you!). And I know that in ten years I'll be ready to write another book all about the crazy ways it will have affected me. But right now I'm hemorrhaging, so I can honestly say that I look forward to a vagina as dry as the Sahara Desert.

The old McCarthyism meant . . . humorlessness

The new McCarthyism means . . . being able to laugh at yourself

The old McCarthyism meant . . . being suspicious of others' motives

The new McCarthyism means . . . never doubting the kindness of strangers

If My Bed Could Talk . . .

"Please flip the mattress. When you actually get lucky with a guy, it's pretty obvious you sleep alone most of the time because he is rolling into the mattress dent you have created."

"Please buy me more than one outfit. You have one set of sheets, yet you own two thousand pairs of shoes."

"When you leave the house, the dog dry-humps me. Get him fixed or get rid of him."

"I can't make myself, so do me a favor and get me dressed before you leave for work. What if *you* had to spend the day with your pants down? Wait . . . never mind."

"You might want to look underneath me if you are missing something. Playing hide-and-seek is the only fun I get to have. So far I'm hiding one earring, two remote controls, one of Evan's shoes, and your 'back massager.'"

"I'm not a maxi pad. Mark a calendar and come to bed prepared, girl!"

"Tell Evan's friend Mikey that I'm not a trampoline. Next time I'm gonna make it hurt."

"You are multitalented: you snore, you fart, and you talk in your sleep."

"Even though boys may come and go, I've got your back, girl. Literally."

Ten Signs You're Spending Too Much Time with Your Toddler

1. You have strong feelings about the way Dora the Explorer treats Boots.

2. Most of the food you eat is off your child's face.

3. There is a Go-Gurt or a juice box in your car door.

4. You haven't had an alcoholic cocktail in two years.

5. You bite someone at Walmart for taking the sale item you wanted.

6. You tell your husband you're not going to blow him unless he eats all his broccoli.

7. You use your spit to wipe something off a friend's face.

8. At the end of the day you're wondering what letter brought the day to you.

9. You wear a macaroni necklace out to dinner.

10. You check your husband's bum to be sure he wiped properly.

Nourish Your Soul

I grew up on the South Side of Chicago, and we liked our meals big in them parts. This was years before serving sizes and processed foods and calorie counting were a big part of the lexicon. Not in my family, anyway. Our test for a meal's worth was portion size. Roadside diners always got high marks; I gained the nickname "Truck Driver" because of the way I could put away the mounds of food they served at their counters.

Later in life, I gained something else: about eighty pounds in pregnancy. I read somewhere that the average weight of checked baggage is fifty pounds, and I can tell you it sure felt as though I was dragging around an extra suitcase or two—on my ass. My high-water mark was 211 pounds. It turned out that Evan's adorable body only accounted for six of them. The other goop that was in there added up to another ten pounds; I left the hospital at 195.

Evan didn't mind my doughy body. He didn't

judge. But producers judge and casting directors judge and magazine editors judge. I don't care what some celebrities say about not paying attention to tabloid headlines—no one *wants* to see her ass or thigh magnified (with a circle or arrow making sure everyone sees the cellulite) on the cover of a magazine. If I was going to stay in show business, I obviously needed to get busy losing some weight.

My mom had had success with Weight Watchers, so I decided to give it a whirl. The portion control portion of the program made sense to me, and I could get my limited brain bandwidth (babies suck the intelligence right out of you) around the point system. I also liked that they didn't overdo the lecture about having to work out as well. I mean, one thing at a time, right? Weight Watchers worked for me. I lost all my baby weight. I even became a spokesperson for the program for a while. I can't argue with the results, even if I often wanted to gnaw off my baby's pudgy arm on days when I'd consumed all my allotted points by 2:00 p.m.

I've also tried a lot of fad diets when I've had to get "red carpet ready" (how I loathe HD—a girl can't get away with anything anymore!). I tend to do a juice cleanse in early January every year even if it seems to make me more toxic . . . to be around, anyway.

On the first day of the cleanse my hunger is predictably persistent but low-grade. I think about food with great fondness; not being able to chew anything makes me a little blue. The second day I am a hangry bitch. For those of you not versed in diet-speak, "hangry" is hungry + angry. In other words, short-tempered, headachy, and *in no mood to deal with your shit.* Day three is supposed to bring me renewed energy and internal lightness, but all I feel is dizzy and disoriented. By day five I'm googling for pictures of food like a porn addict. Every year I swear I won't do this again, but every year I do it anyway.

More recently I've discovered something totally, mind-blowingly, life-alteringly revolutionary: vegetables fill my belly without making my butt big. I can eat them to my heart's content and the only thing I might get is gassy.

Not news to you? Well, when I was growing up, the potato was the only vegetable we ate regularly (fried, baked, mashed, and hashed), so you'll have to forgive my awe and excitement over the variety now available in the produce aisle. With the range of color, shapes, and sizes, it's like the bra and panty section in department stores. Vegetables like carrots and broccoli and peas are the equivalent of granny panties—familiar, comfortable, and easy to put on (the table). Artichokes and eggplant and fennel? More like silky lingerie—I eat/wear them often but not so much that they become uninteresting. Then there are the more exotic vegetables—kohlrabi, bok choy, or mustard greens—that are kind of like the Swarovski-bedazzled bras and thongs only available at the Victoria's Secret runway show. Pull those out on rare, rare occasions and wow someone with your ability to rock his world!

The most nutritious, generally low-calorie, and easiest way to make any vegetable into a meal? Put it into a pot with some broth and a protein and *ba-bam*— soup. Another earth-shattering revelation for me!

I know what you're thinking: soup is a watery appetizer, the skippable section of restaurant menus. Until I began experimenting with soup, I would have agreed with you. But now soup works for me on so many levels. There's the one-pot thing, for starters. You can make vats of it and not dirty a lot of pots and pans. Almost all soups freeze well—perfect for people like me who only want to devote one afternoon to stocking up on what I'll eat for the whole week. And there's the fact that my energy level is way up and my weight has stayed down while I've been eating as much soup as I could ever want. Oh, and eat soup regularly and you'll be regular: my bowels are in the best shape of my life.

I know this is getting a little carried away with the metaphor, but the humble soup is a lot like life. Good soups use simple, basic ingredients, are easy to modify with whatever you happen to have in your own personal pantry, most often get better with age (more flavor with each passing day), and can not only feed large gatherings of people but also nourish the soul. I have stacks of one-serving containers of my homemade frozen soups in my cold, cold Chicago garage. People beg me for my recipes! Maybe I'll have to write that book next. . . . For now, here are two of my favorite veggie soup recipes.

CARROT GINGER

Ingredients:

½-inch finger of ginger, peeled and sliced paper thin

⅓ cup hot water

1 medium onion, chopped

1 garlic clove

½ tablespoon olive oil

¼ pound carrots, peeled and diced

4 cups chicken or vegetable stock

1 teaspoon salt

¼ teaspoon black pepper

Directions:

Steep ginger in the hot water for approximately 30 minutes, then strain out the ginger pieces and reserve the water.

Sweat the garlic and onion in the oil until translucent.

Add carrots and sweat for another five minutes, stirring occasionally.

Add the stock to the pot, bring to a boil and then reduce to simmer until the carrots are fork tender.

Add the ginger water to the pot.

Puree the soup and season to taste with salt and pepper.

NO-CREAM OF BROCCOLI

■ ■

Ingredients:

2 tablespoons Not-Butter Earth Balance Spread

1 onion, roughly chopped

2 garlic cloves, minced

½ tablespoon olive oil

4 cups chicken or vegetable stock

1 head broccoli with most of the stems trimmed
   off

1 russet potato, peeled and roughly chopped

1 teaspoon salt

¼ teaspoon black pepper

Directions:

Lightly sauté the onions and garlic in the oil until translucent.

Add the broccoli florets and the potato, sauté for about 5 minutes.

Add the stock and continue to simmer until the broccoli and potatoes are tender.

Puree the soup and season to taste with salt and pepper.

How to Get Souper Skinny

f I ever write a book about staying thin, getting in shape, or being in the "optimal wellness zone" (does anyone really know what those books are about?), I would call it *The Souper Skinny Soup Diet Cookbook.* All of my recipes would be gluten- and dairy-free. That is, mostly fart-free. Here are some I might include:

It's All Nasty

A playful twist on Gwyneth's preciously packaged, über-healthy, gold-plated cooking style. (Chef's tip: stock up on air freshener for the bathroom before making this deliciously perfect pipe cleaner!)

Rehab with Lindsay Lohan

A colon-cleansing concoction that draws heavily on detoxifying herbs and veggies to clean out the garbage truck your body has become.

Here Comes the Bridesmaid

A lean and green version of Italian wedding soup (that is, no meatballs, lots of kale), tailored to help you lose weight quickly but not harshly. It'll also give your complexion an antioxidant-fueled glow, so you'll look great in your BFF's wedding photos (though not in that atrocious dress!).

Countdown to Vegas, Bitches (alternative title: High School Reunion: Take a Look at Me Now, Queen Bees!)

When you've got only about six weeks to get your bod ready for its close-up, this pea-based soup is just the ticket! It's a moderately fast fat burner. You'll lose weight without losing your mind. (Chef's note: This soup can't protect your mind once you're in Las Vegas, but at least your ass will look good.)

No, I'm Not Pregnant, You Asshole

Nothing's worse than being taken for someone who's seven months pregnant. Nothing. This waist-whittling white-bean-and-broccoli preparation will help you lose weight at a sane pace, with the added benefit of giving you the kind of gas that will shut everyone up.

Ten Signs You Need
My Cookbook

Wondering whether you are in need of my weight-loss cookbook (see page 83)? Here are some clear indications that it would be a good idea:

1. You think you find a new mole on your boob, but it's a Raisinet.

2. You eat the warm boob Raisinet.

3. You wear yoga pants everywhere except to do yoga.

4. You eat Lean Cuisine meals as snacks.

5. You try the dog's food because it smells so good. Mmmm, *bacon*!

6. You think you may have a thyroid condition.

7. You drive back to a fast-food restaurant because they forgot your sauce.

8. Every time you go grocery shopping they have to ring up at least two empty containers of something.

9. You burn your mouth at least once a week.

10. You ate your edible underwear.

Know When to Fold 'Em

> ## RECIPE FOR SUCCESS
>
> ■ ■ ■ ■ ■ ■ ■ ■ ■ ■ ■ ■ ■ ■ ■ ■ ■ ■
>
> **Ingredients:**
>
> *3 cups gut instinct*
>
> *A long, hard look in the mirror*
>
> *The willingness to pay attention to what your gut*
> *instinct or the mirror is trying to tell you*
>
> *1 girlfriend who will confirm your gut instinct or be*
> *your mirror*
>
> *"The Gambler" on your playlist*

When Evan was ten, we were away on vacation and he suddenly announced that he wanted to break up with his girlfriend. I had known the relationship was doomed (I mean, everything she wore—right down to her shoelaces—was Hello Kitty), but I wanted to hear his reasoning anyway. "Out of sight, out of mind," he explained. He had been apart from her all of five days. I had to give him an A for honesty.

Many men seem to want to have their cake and eat it, too. Or, more accurately, to have their Hello Kitty and eat someone else's pussy, too. We girlfriends and wives know this in theory but we never think *our* guy has the cheating gene. That crap behavior is for other women's dickhead men.

There are signs, of course. Longer and more excited stories about his day, filled with details designed to throw you off the scent. Or a burst of out-of-the-blue accusatory anger—you say something as simple as "Did you remember the orange juice?" and he screams back, "Juice? Is that all I am around here? Someone to buy juice? Get your own damn OJ!"

Too often, even when you have an inkling and home in on those signs, you won't believe it until you have concrete proof of his infidelity. I don't blame you—no one really wants to believe that her man is straying. Admitting it means you have to do something about it. From where you sit, it's just going to take too much emotional energy to rock the boat by tossing him out or walking out yourself. And the thought of being alone again? Ugh! I know, denial is much more pleasant. For a while, anyway (see below).

It's funny what can finally make each of us snap. It's usually such a small, small thing. The kind of thing that leaves your friends scratching their heads: "*That's* the thing that made the difference?" they say. But it's meaningful to you for some reason, and whatever it is, it puts you on a new life course. You can't take one more minute of this bullshit.

About ten years ago a friend of mine co-wrote a book called *He's Just Not That Into You*. If you weren't paying attention or didn't yet know how to read back then, allow me to summarize for you: it told us (women) what they (men) really think about some relationships and why they do what they do (and don't do). A couple of weeks after its publication, a whole nation of doors slammed at once as readers saw themselves on the pages and finally got the hell out of crap relationships. Another way to put it is that knowing when to hold 'em or when to fold 'em, knowing when to walk away and when to run (any Kenny Rogers fans out there? I know you're humming!) is what separates the women from the girls, and a lot of girls became women that year.

Among the epiphanies:

He's just not that into you if . . . he's married to someone else.

He's just not that into you if . . . he only calls you at 3:00 a.m. for sex.

He's just not that into you if . . . he doesn't want you
to meet his friends.

Duh, right? But I'm willing to bet that almost everyone has at some point been this level of abso-
fucking-lutely blind. The (hypothetical) wack logic
goes something like this:

It wasn't really cheating when he slept with that other
girl because we hadn't officially become girlfriend
and boyfriend . . . even though we were kind of living together.

Well, I did make him sit through *Pretty Woman* when
I had food poisoning last month, so he deserved a
night out with the boys at a strip club in Reno.

My family really can be a pain in the ass, so it's okay if
he doesn't go with me to my sister's wedding and
plays Xbox with his friends instead.

If I ever heard a friend say any of the above, I'd tell
her to get her head out of her ass. When I was much
younger, they had to do the same for me on occasion.
Maybe you'd find a more diplomatic way to set her
straight. If so, you're a kinder, gentler friend than me
and mine. But we get the job done faster!

Of course, *hearing* what my friend's book or your inner voice or your friend or Kenny Rogers is saying is different from *listening* to what they have to say. You might pay lip service to the advice and vow to make a change. But it's no easy or quick task to actually change. Trimming the fat, lightening your load, getting real, treating yourself well: these Hallmarky goals are not simple to achieve. It's a sometimes painful process, and it usually mimics the five stages of grief.

You start in *denial*—you're in the trenches and you'll do almost anything to justify sticking with it:

Your guy periodically comes home late and smelling like cheap perfume, but you're willing to believe his story that he's been trying to secretly learn to tango so he can surprise you next time on the dance floor. You continue to believe this explanation (and are touched by his thoughtfulness) even when he still can't dance for shit.

You find burner phones in the glove box of his car, and when you press redial on one, you get the front desk at a cheap motel just off the highway near your house. You are more willing to believe he's selling drugs (which you also don't want to deal with) than that he might be stopping by for a quickie on his way home.

If you've acknowledged his shortcomings, you tell yourself he's not *that* bad. If you've busted him in a lie, you believe him that it was just that once. Or you convince yourself that another woman is to blame for his cheating heart. Or you *just know* he'll change because you are sure you can change him. See wack logic above. Translation: however shitty he might be, he's someone, and someone is better than no one.

The denial stage is so twisted and protracted that you might even convince yourself that wanting to be with a turd rather than be alone shows a remarkable depth of self-understanding. You might even pat yourself on the back for making that "breakthrough." If you listen carefully, however, you'll also hear a tiny little voice telling you that you would be okay on your own, even if you're afraid to try it. That's your self-worth struggling to be heard, ladies. Stop turning the radio up to drown it out! Get your head out of your ass!

After the absurdity of your justification starts to dawn on you, humiliation might set in. And your embarrassment quickly tips you over into the second stage: *anger*. Now maybe you can say, "He's a mother-fucking two-timing asshole, and I am going to hunt him down and chop his balls off." Or you announce, "I am not going to waste another day on that worthless piece of shit," and you toss all his things out the window (if he ever left anything after a booty call) and change the locks on your apartment door for good measure. You rage at him, at yourself, at the world. Maybe you even start up with someone new to make him jealous. When that doesn't work, you get madder (and now maybe you've got the added problem of a new relationship you'll have to get out of).

Whether anger works on him or not—maybe he'll come back with his tail between his legs, or maybe he'll say, "Fine, see ya!"—you're probably soon going to find yourself in the pathetic phase of *bargaining*, when you're willing to compromise to keep his love. God help you, you start to backpedal: "Maybe if I can learn to need less than the little I needed before, I could make it work again." Or "If he would just show me a sign, I'd make him a key for that new lock on my apartment door."

Then even you can't stand to listen to yourself grasp at straws, and it dawns on you that there is no going back. *Depression* strikes! "What an idiot I am for ever thinking this would work out. I've wasted three years of my life on that loser. I need to sleep for a month, but I'll probably feel just as sucky when I wake up. This is hopeless."

Unless you are now clinically depressed and need

meds to jump-start your climb back to a healthier emotional state (no shame in that), the clouds will eventually start to part and you will now finally, finally have come to some level of *acceptance*. What a relief it is when you finally have the lady balls to stand up for yourself and say clearly, "I'm not okay with the way he treated me or made me feel." And mean it!

When you have reached the acceptance phase, you have likely also gained precious perspective. Maybe you can now say, "I am detaching with love (and a healthy amount of resentment that I'll work through with a therapist for the next few years) and acknowledging that he-who-shall-remain-nameless and I were not meant for the long haul." You see the bad relationship for what it was, see the part you played in keeping it alive (even if everyone else thought it was really only on life support), and want better for yourself the next time around. That's not only reading the signs but learning to follow their directions as well. And you'll be a better partner for that gained knowledge (see page 107 for my genius advice on being a better partner). You'll attract a better caliber of human being the next time around. Maybe only a slightly better caliber, but every gained inch counts.

(I'm talking about baby steps toward better choices, not dick length, in case there was any confusion there!)

If you don't recognize yourself in the wack logic above, good for you. But the central message of *He's Just Not That Into You* can be applied to other areas of your life as well.

For example, if you're not getting promoted at work year after year (and assuming you're working your ass off), then your job is just not that into you. Dust off your résumé and start looking for an employer that appreciates you more.

If your roommate is always messy and shorts you on her half of the rent, then your roomie's just not that into you. Make plans to move on and in with someone who doesn't take your cleaning skills and bank account for granted.

Those old pants that always crawl inside your ass? Those pants are *in* you but just not that *into* you! That suit jacket with the shoulder pads, the one that makes you look like a linebacker? Not only is it not into you, but it's completely not in. Toss those old clothes and find a new style!

Ten Signs the Guy You're Dating Is Too Young for You

1. He owns a skateboard.

2. He knows his top score at anything.

3. He thinks weed is a staple food.

4. He owns a cape.

5. He's never washed his own sheets.

6. He air-dries when his towel is too dirty.

7. He calls you "dude."

8. You're older than his parents.

9. He can't name any roles Hugh Jackman has played other than Wolverine.

10. He thinks "you're" is spelled "ur."

Six Signs You Might Not Have Chemistry in Bed with Your Partner

1. He tells you he's not really into blow jobs.

2. If the phone rings, you both agree someone should get it.

3. The dirtiest thing you say to him in bed is "Did you take a shower today?"

4. Whenever you're naked he giggles.

5. When's he's done he rolls over and says, "All righty, then!"

6. And one very obvious sign that you don't have chemistry: you flinch every time he touches you.

Ten Signs the Guy You're Dating Might Be Gay

1. He thinks you're fabulous.

2. He thinks your shoes are fierce.

3. He thinks your face is *gorge*.

4. He knows who Liza Minnelli is and can sing at least two of her songs.

5. He does your makeup for every event.

6. When you plan your future together, he sketches your wedding dress.

7. He thinks you look great in magenta.

8. He knows what magenta is.

9. He wants to paint an accent wall in your apartment.

10. Every time you get in a fight, he cries.

Eight Signs You Might Be Stalking Your Ex

1. You own night-vision goggles.

2. You find hope and hear an emphasis on the word "think" when he says "I don't *think* I can see you anymore."

3. When he tells you you're the craziest person he's ever dated, you think, "I'm special."

4. You think "Don't call me anymore" means just for today.

5. You read the horoscopes for both of you and take them literally.

6. You still talk to his mom.

7. You tattoo his name on your back for fun.

8. You tell his new girlfriend you have herpes.

A Short Course on Being—and Attracting—Someone Special

After you've clawed your way through the five stages of grief that often accompany ditching an asshole (see page 93), you may be gun-shy about dipping your toe in the dating/getting-naked pool again. Then again, you may have gotten involved with someone new as a crutch to help you ditch the asshole in the first place. And that's often effective, I've got to admit.

But is it wise? Are you serving yourself well (not to mention this new guy) by not examining the pattern of your mistakes or really giving yourself time to heal before coupling up again? I'm just sayin'.

But let's assume you've done a little soul-searching and you're feeling ready. Maybe so ready (aka horny) that you want to cannonball into the deep end of the pool. Great! Being afraid of failure would be way worse. But may I make a few suggestions? Through trial (lots), error (too many to count), and a very tall stack of self-help books, I have boiled things down to the five essential mantras that follow. These mantras are all ways of behaving lovingly toward another person, and if you live and date by them, you're going to be one hell of a catch! They are also ways of behaving lovingly toward *yourself.*

Be Conscious

Part of the fun of falling for someone new is that floaty, detached-from-the-real-world feeling, and you shouldn't deny yourself that dreamy time. But you can be dreamy and conscious at the same time. I'm talking about being aware of your decisions and how they can affect people you love, including yourself. Be mindful with your words, both the hurtful ones and the loving ones (you can give "I love you" away too soon), your actions, and the consequences of both. Then ask yourself this question: is he doing the same?

Be Vulnerable

No one wants to be with a cocky a-hole. At least not for long. (At first there's a certain something about cocky bastards, isn't there? Ya, I'll give you that.) So try not to be one. When you open your heart and let down your guard, allowing your new guy to see the parts of your mind (and body) you don't share with the world, you give the relationship a chance to deepen. And again, ask yourself this question: is he reciprocating?

Be Transparent

Crazy-sexy, filmy lingerie is not what I'm talking about! Being transparent with someone means that you are striving for clear and honest communication. No mixed signals! If you've got insecurities (who doesn't?) or have brought emotional baggage into this relationship (see "Don't Past-Project" on page 111), you are at least trying to own up to it. Say it with me now: does he try to do the same for you?

RECIPE FOR DISASTER: THE MIXED-SIGNAL COCKTAIL

Ingredients:

1 man who wants his woman to read his mind, isn't saying what he means, or is bringing assumptions to a conversation that have more to do with past experiences than the reality of the present moment

1 woman who wants her man to read her mind, isn't saying what she means, or is bringing assumptions to a conversation that have more to do with past experiences than with the reality of the present moment,

1 conversation about any of the following:

- What to do this weekend. (He says: "Do you want to come to a party with me? I'm cool with it if you don't want to, but let's meet up afterward anyway." You hear: "I'm not ready to bring you as my girlfriend, so I hope you don't want to come . . . but I do want some booty late at night." What he *might* have meant: "I have to go, but I think it's going to be a sucky party. I want to save you the

hassle and I can leave early to meet you somewhere else.")

- What you'd like for your birthday. (You say: "Really, I don't want or need anything!" He hears: "Really, I don't want or need anything!" What you
might have meant: "I think it's selfish and greedy
to ask for anything, but I really hope you do something special for me!")

- Whether he thinks the woman at the next table is
attractive. (He says: "Yes, but not in *that* way and
she doesn't compare to you!" You hear: "I can't
take my eyes off her, so I will overcompensate by
complimenting you." What he *might* have meant:
"I only have eyes for you. Really.")

Directions:
Shake well and don't expect a good outcome.

Don't Past-Project

This is a fancy shrink way of saying you need to remember whom you are dealing with. This new guy is
not the dude who hurt you badly all those years ago (or
just last week). The guy who hurt you is in the past

(right?), so leave him there. The only reason to ever go back to the past is to heal it, but do that with a therapist or a good friend. The new guy is not the person to process all that with.

Be Faithful

If the a-hole you had to ditch was a cheater, then you know firsthand how bad it feels to be cheated on, right? If you've never been cheated on, then let me tell you what the rest of the world knows: you shouldn't wish it on your worst enemy. Being the cheater eats away at your soul (if you've got a soul at all), and if the other person has a nasty STD, the cheating could eat away at your body, too! If you want to play the field, do it honestly; make it clear you're not interested in monogamy and let him decide for himself if he wants to stick around. Expect the same directness in return.

If you're not ready to date again, consider getting a dog. After all . . .

- You can lock him in the bathroom if he humps your friends.

- You can blame your gas on him.

- You can have his balls removed legally.

- If needed, you can muzzle him.

- If you throw up, he will clean it up for you.

My Wet Dreams

can bring home the bacon, fry it up in a pan, and never, never, never let you forget you're a man! Am I completely dating myself to ask if you remember that little jingle from the Enjoli perfume ad of the 1970s? Well, Google it if you don't know it. And be prepared to laugh.

Though I can indeed bring home the bacon, fry it up in a pan, and never, never, never let my man forget he's a man . . . I'm exhausted. Aren't you?

An average working day (one that doesn't include long-distance travel, an evening event, a photo shoot, or a publisher meeting) for me begins at 5:00 a.m. and ends around 11:00 p.m. I spend a lot of time taking care of Evan—getting him ready for his day, cooking for him, and helping him with his homework. I spend a lot of time in a car getting to and from work. I spend a lot of time *at* work. And answering phone calls and emails.

Like anyone else, I pick up around the house, go to

the grocery store, sort the mail, and pay the bills. In my "free" time I blog, write an advice column, and write books. I also like to throw a love life in there, and that takes time and energy.

Some days I'm really on my game, don't piss anyone off, take A+ care of my son, and can bring a little Playmate to my romantic relationship. Other days, not so much—I'm impatient and overextended, and I'm lucky if I can keep up with Evan's play*dates*.

I know I shouldn't complain. I can afford help with some of these tasks, and I usually take a car service to and from work instead of battling traffic from behind the wheel myself (but I work in New York City so I don't really have a choice). Through my work, I get to meet a lot of smart and famous people. Sometimes the people are both of these things (but brains and fame don't always go together). And I've got my health, so I'm thankful. (Health is one thing, looks are another. As I get older I have to spend an increasing amount of time trying to look younger, which sucks, but my sisters tell me I'm looking more and more like Jimmy Carter so I've got to do something.) But the exhaustion . . . it's brutal. To reference another old ad, I swear that sometimes I just want to yell, "Calgon, take me away!" To lie back in a massive bathtub with acres of soothing, fragrant bubbles and hot, hot water and let *someone else be me.* That's my kind of wet dream (pun intended).

I also often wonder what it would be like to have someone else's life. A simpler, less public one. Like, maybe, the life of a high school guidance counselor?

Seriously, that's an advice giver's fantasy job. You sit in your cute little office—which is decorated cheerily with a positive-affirmation-a-day desk calendar and encouraging comic strips posted on the cork bulletin board above the computer screen—and you chat with and cheer up teenagers whose biggest problem is the C+ they are getting in physics or not making the varsity cheerleading squad. (*Poor babies!* Remember when life was *that* simple?) You go to faculty meetings where you can nap without anyone noticing. Plus, the school day is over around three, so if need be, you can hit several happy hours on the way home to wash away any aggravations of the day. And summers off? Dreamy!

Wait, but what if I misdiagnose garden-variety teenage funk and miss the signs of threatened suicide? How would I say something new and convincing in every college recommendation I'm asked to write? Would all the people I meet be interesting, or would some be angry, worried, and helicoptering parents? Oh, and what about having to fend off pervy advances from the PE teacher? And all that advice giving doesn't leave much time for online poker. And I'd probably have to spend my summers catching up on sleep and getting up the nerve to go back to work in September (which probably ruins all of August). I wouldn't have a car service and likely wouldn't get to wear as many cute clothes. Okay, not the most perfect job after all. Sounds just as chaotic and stressful as my chosen path. Maybe more so. Sorry, guidance counselors of the world. Hang in there!

I once worked in this great little Polish grocery in Chicago. That's a good job. Talk about not having to bring your work home with you. Punch in, punch lots of buttons, punch out. No stress, no mess. Behind a cash register, there is no chaos. There's a shiny button for everything, and it makes a sound to let you know you've made the correct choice.

I even went to work there on acid twice. That's the sign of a radically great job—you can do it just fine while being higher than Mount Everest.

I loved selling Lotto tickets (and booze to minors; they are always so grateful!). I loved counting change back to customers, but if I was feeling lazy, the register would do that work for me and tell me exactly how much to give back. I loved trying to figure out how best to pack someone's groceries in the fewest number of bags without the bags getting so heavy they'd break (so much easier than figuring out how to stuff my own body into shapewear that won't smash my boobs).

I even liked the crabby customers. Because grocery store customers complain about the price of produce and dog food, the weather, insufficient parking spaces, traffic, and shampoo that makes their hair fall out. They don't complain about you not having enough time for them. They never ask you to change so that you'll be "more appealing to viewers." They don't expect more from you than you are already giving.

Of course, there were downsides to being a cashier. There was the fear of robbery to contend with (made more alarming on acid), shoplifters, and the dreaded bathroom mop-out every few hours. And clock punching isn't everything it's cracked up to be in terms of salary. I do remember that.

I guess I'll go back to being me.

RECIPE FOR SUCCESS

Ingredients:

1 job you like well enough

At least 2 people you can lean on

1 very deep bathtub with Jacuzzi jets

Fun fantasies that remind you to be grateful for

what you've already got

Ten Signs You're Getting Older

1. You reference decades-old TV ads when telling stories or giving advice (see page 115).

2. Separate beds make sense to you.

3. Going to bed is your favorite part of each day.

4. You get a charley horse making love.

5. You can't walk up two flights of stairs without needing a break.

6. You consider wrapping packs of gum as Christmas presents.

7. You watch church on TV on Sunday instead of going.

8. You have no idea what a fourteen-year-old is saying to you.

9. You will make a line of people wait while you count out exact change.

10. You can't talk your way out of a traffic ticket.

When All Else Fails . . .
Have an Orgasm for the Soul

RECIPE FOR SUCCESS

■ ■ ■ ■ ■ ■ ■ ■ ■ ■ ■ ■ ■ ■ ■ ■ ■ ■ ■

Ingredients:

10 minutes to yourself

A secluded place or a soundproof room

1 box of tissues (or the hem of your dress or the
*   sleeve of your shirt)*

No access to social media

When I can't fantasize my way out of a bad day, my preferred coping method is to clench my butt cheeks, square my shoulders, plaster a big smile on my face, and breathe deeply. Making lists to prioritize what's on my plate can stabilize me. Chocolate-covered anything helps. So does repeating the mantra "This too shall pass."

Which was working well enough one busy, stressful day until I found myself at Trader Joe's getting wine and peanut butter pretzels after work. The pimply cashier (who was no doubt busy enjoying his stress-free day; see page 118) said, "Hey, I know you . . . oh no, maybe not. Forget it, you are way too old to be her." Did that mean he thought I was me, but that my up-close face didn't match the Jenny McCarthy he'd seen on TV? Or did it mean he thought I resembled another actress—Jennie Garth, maybe?—but that my clearly advanced age made it impossible I could be her? However you interpret the comment, it was no compliment. He'd just told me I looked old.

Look, it'd be the pot calling the kettle black for sure if I were to suggest that we shouldn't speak our minds. I make my living stating my opinion on national TV; I certainly enjoy the freedom of speech. But had no one told this kid to not say out loud everything that crossed his mind? That telling a woman she looks old is really, really impolite?

You'd think I'd have a thicker skin, but I'd had a crap day and something about that offhand and un-kind remark just unhinged me. I could see the *Star* headline: "Jenny McCarthy Loses It Buying a Case of Two-Buck Chuck." I couldn't risk tears in public (a hazard of a publicly lived life), so I left the wine and the pretzels and ran from the store. I must have looked a little out of my mind, waving my hand around and desperately jabbing the button on my keys to try to make the lock chirp that would remind me where I'd parked my car.

The parking lot was crowded, and I could see the telltale glimmer of recognition in more than a few pairs of eyes. *If there is any God at all,* I thought, *they too will think I'm Jennie Garth, and she and her aging will become the cocktail party gossip this weekend instead of the behavior being attributed to me!*

My car wasn't cooperating—no chirp chirp. I hadn't had a good cry in so long that I couldn't be sure how big the tsunami would be if I unleashed it. So I panicked. I ran down the street, wild-eyed, looking for a place I could hide.

I knew there was a park a couple of blocks away and sprinted toward it. This involved crossing a major street and therefore a good number of supportive messages yelled to me out the windows of air-conditioned cars and over squealing brakes. This was Los Angeles, after all, and Angelenos are known for their patience and kindness behind the wheel.

Gasping for breath, I got to the park and looked around for a secluded bench. Bad luck. This being Los Angeles, every bench or patch of grass was already occupied by homeless people stroking mangy cats and/or arguing with imaginary friends. I couldn't hang on one second more. So I let it rip. Right there in the open. I burst into tears and shook my fists at the sky. I walked back and forth listing all the reasons why my life sucked, in between new bouts of wailing.

One benchwarmer who wore a rope for a belt, one red mitten, and a toothless grin yelled, "Keep going, sister. You tell 'em. You tell 'em good." It was the most supportive thing I had heard all week. Which only made me cry harder.

Because I've since bothered to look into it, I now know that I was just about to experience a physiological phenomenon not unlike having an orgasm. Crying, it turns out, releases endorphins, which will ultimately make you feel better. Exhausted, too, but a peaceful, satisfied exhaustion, like after a productive roll in the sheets.

And that's what happened. After a few minutes of bone-rattling sobbing, the waterworks slowed down to a trickle. I paced a little more and wiped my snot with my sleeve. I calmed down. I felt just a little bit refreshed. The drama passed, and I regained a little bit of perspective. Old to the little prick at Trader Joe's probably meant twenty-five, I reminded myself. And I'd bet that actresses older than me get that kind of double take, too, and maybe someone tells them they couldn't be Jenny McCarthy because they are just too

old to be me. I'll bet Suzanne Somers gets that sometimes, and she's the poster woman for aging gracefully
and happily and sexily. I saw a little ray of sunshine
push through my cloudy mood.

My friend with the red mitten saw it, too. She
called out to me, "That's better, girl. You tell 'em good.
I think you should have won that dance thing on the
TV for sure."

The Jennie Garth mistake again. "You're confusing
me with someone else," I started to say proudly. But
then I thought, *Screw it. At least she didn't think I was
Jimmy Carter!*

When you really do need to wallow in your sorrows
and self-pity just a little longer, put on a pair of
stretchy pants, mix up a batch of my Pity Party Mix,
and indulge.

PITY PARTY MIX

Ingredients:

2 cups Bugles

2 cups White Cheddar Cheez-Its

2 cups Glutino Pretzels

2 cups Cap'n Crunch with or without Crunch Ber-
  ries (ladies' choice)
2 cups popcorn
2 cups Lucky Charms
2 bags white chocolate chips or white almond
  bark

Directions:
Toss the first six ingredients together. Melt white chocolate chips or almond bark and toss the dry ingredients in it until coated. If you can stand to, spread the mix on wax paper to allow the chocolate to harden. Then chow down. If you can't wait for the chocolate to harden, periodically wipe your hands on those awesome stretch pants. If there is any left over (unlikely), store in an airtight container until your next meltdown.

Date Night Etiquette

1. We all see the occasional Facebook posts that say "Date Night!!" Don't be that asshole. Keep it to yourself.

2. Don't post or tweet *during* date night. You are supposed to be focused on the person across the table from you, idiot.

3. Go to a family-*un*friendly restaurant. If they have a kids' menu (or if the chef is willing to serve the homemade pasta with just butter and cheese), you have failed.

4. Swear. Cuss like a sailor. Get it all out while you can. If anyone within earshot has a problem with it, throw your butter knife at them.

5. After dinner, have sex in a cheap motel or in the backseat of your car. You run the risk of getting a

binky or animal crackers stuck in your crack, but who cares? You're getting laid in a location that is not your boring bed.

6. Don't keep checking your phone to see if the babysitter has called. Your kids are fine. They're probably asleep or eating candy while the babysitter is texting friends to come over and drink all your vodka. All's well.

7. Discuss ahead of time who will talk to and pay the babysitter when you get home. The person who pulls the short straw on this should stop drinking a little early. There is nothing worse than slurring to your sitter. Driving home drunk is bad, too.

8. If your babysitter doesn't have her own transportation, spend a little extra to arrange for her to get a cab or car service home. You certainly don't want to drive her home in the car you've just bonked in.

Reverse Psychology

They say that good thoughts do more than just distract you from bad things—they can also attract good things.

And we're told—even from a very young age—that compassion toward others breeds kindness in return. That whole Golden Rule thing, you know?

Any and every guru worth his or her salt would argue that satisfaction in life comes from enjoying the present moment for what it is, not dwelling on the past, fixating on the future, or fretting over what others have that you do not.

Scientists even point out that optimism makes new neural pathways in your brain! (I read *Psychology Today* when I'm waiting at the gyno, too, you know.)

Why then, with all the evidence about the power of positive thinking and the great things that can come of great behavior, are pessimism and pettiness the default temperament for so many? I mean, could there be an evolutionary benefit to negativity? OMG—I may be on to something now!

(Even if science can't prove that particular theory, there is a whole lot of evidence that bad things happen all the time to good people, which proves the legitimacy of negative assumptions and defeatist thinking. So there.)

I have my own fun little theory. I believe that there is a certain magic, a powerful power, in negative thinking. So many of us "go there" because it obviously gives us something we can't get anywhere else: the sweet, sweet comfort of denial. The kind that ostriches must get when they bury their heads in the sand. If harnessed correctly, it can take you places that optimism and positivity never could. Backward in emotional development, for instance—how cool is that? It also ages you quickly—something everyone strives for!

Let's look at the many other advantages of negative personality traits (but be careful; these things can become addictive).

The Benefits of Bitterness

Bitterness is one of the few emotions you can actually taste in your mouth, so don't undervalue it. It's powerful medicine! Being bitter—whether it's about other people's success or their possessions or their whole damn lucky life—is a super-duper, fast-acting, go-to defense mechanism. Bitterness helps you sleep at night, tucked in warm and cozy with the knowledge that others are not nearly as deserving as you; they obviously just slept with someone at the top.

Bitterness is an especially handy tool when you feel like ranting and raving about someone else's entitled attitude and unearned success (which is an approach to life that's obviously so much less self-aware than your own bitter state of mind). See reference to Paris Hilton and Kim Kardashian on the next page.

The Upside of Entitlement

The only thing faster-acting than believing that hard work and talent don't pay off is the belief that even if they do, you deserve a shortcut around all the effort.

I had an assistant once who, just three months into the job with me (and not too much longer than that out of college), presented me with a written plan to become my business partner and start pulling in a six-figure salary, plus bonuses based on *my* work. At the time I thought this was the equivalent of speeding past the long line of cars on a highway off-ramp and then cutting in without even an embarrassed blinker at the last minute (Jesus, that makes me mad). And I still like that analogy. But now I think this would-be executive was on to something, don't you agree? Talk about brass balls! And initiative! I was presented with a written plan, for God's sake. Paris Hilton and Kim Kardashian never worked so hard to work so little. (See "The Benefits of Bitterness" on page 132.) Too bad—I fired the kid anyway.

The Power of Being Obsessed with the Past

If rehashing your past—whether it's your hurts or your golden days—weren't so therapeutic, there wouldn't be therapists (or career bartenders). There is a certain emotional blissfulness in never mustering the energy to get past your past (or feeling the need to do so). If you are past-obsessive, don't change! Don't stop assuming that the past will repeat itself and that you are powerless to have any impact on your future. Take refuge in the past and you are protected from any future growth. Phew!

The Fruits of Being Obsessed with the Future

If you're not past-obsessive, there's still hope for you. You can skip the present and escape the now in the other direction. Focusing relentlessly on getting somewhere that is not where you are today—at the expense of present-day enjoyment—is a fantastic use of your time and your energies. Add obsessive competitiveness to the mix and you will be the neighborhood champion: you will own more than the Joneses will ever own, your holiday lights will be brighter, you'll have more glamorous parties, and don't even get me started on how your kids will crush everyone in the college admissions wars (whether they want to go to college or not, dammit).

The Judiciousness of Judging Others

The fancy shrink term for what you're doing when you judge or criticize others is "projected identification." In effect, this means that when you feel bad about yourself and don't know what to do with it, you project it onto other people. If you're lucky, you can probably get away with feeling superior without self-awareness. (If you're unlucky, you vaguely understand what you're doing and see the shadow of your own faults in your criticism of others.) It'll help keep you sharp if you practice judging harshly and often. Either way, you get so much off your chest, so keep up the good work.

The Importance of Impatience

Impatience is a terrific stress reliever and blood pressure reducer. I mean, time doesn't grow on trees, and it's not going to slow down just because the lady in line ahead of you has to count out her change (see "Ten Signs You're Getting Older," page 121). Nothing feels better than loudly and frequently expressing your displeasure with everyone else's pace. Who cares that your impatience ratchets up everyone else's stress? Pounding on the dashboard when you're stuck in traffic lets off *your* steam; you don't have time to worry about your passenger's feelings, anyway!

The Rightness of Righteousness

Some say that knowing you're right, that everyone else is mistaken, and that God is definitely on your side is no way to go through life. Clearly, I disagree. It's such a liberating outlook—you can go about your business without a worry in the world. People are just jealous of your confidence, that's all.

The Beauty of Blame

Do you find yourself coming up with excuses as to why it's not your fault when the shit hits the fan? How often do you hold yourself accountable? If your answers are "hell yes" and "never ever," then you are a major-league blamer. The benefits of this state of mind are so obvious I really don't need to list them. Talk about blissful ignorance! Personal accountability is so overrated.

The Blessing of Narcissism

Kanye West really is God's gift to the planet. Need I say more?

STAY THE COURSE

Don't be fooled by the optimists and the kind-hearted, evolved people in your life. If you find yourself being swayed by their rainbows and crystals and yoga chanting, hit the brakes. Trust me, I've driven down that road before. Sometimes I'm still tempted to pull on my driving gloves, throw caution to the wind, and drive on the positive side of the road, but then I remember what I already know, which is that negative thinking trumps positive thinking any day. Take it from a committed negative thinker: the positive road may look beautiful and tree-lined, but a little farther down it becomes a deadly serpentine of zigzags covered in slick black ice.

TED Yourself

RECIPE FOR SUCCESS

■ ■ ■ ■ ■ ■ ■ ■ ■ ■ ■ ■ ■ ■ ■ ■ ■ ■ ■

Ingredients:

At least 1 idea or mission (good, viable, hare-
brained, or insane)

1 cup conviction

1 cup clarity of vision

3 fantasies

1 stage (real or imagined)

Directions:

Practice making your pitch in twenty words or less. Then expand to two minutes. Then indulge in twenty minutes. Even when you have mastered your pitch, be sure to check for accuracy by revisiting and re-vising regularly.

f you've ever tried to pitch a concept—whether it's for a movie, a TV show, an ad campaign, a book, a magazine article, or an innovative line of flea-repellent dog sweaters (and that list is not in order of importance)—you know that getting green-lighted depends largely on your ability to persuade. (That egg-nog latte creamer pitch must have been off-the-charts persuasive, huh? See page 42.)

On the face of it, what makes something persuasive is hard to put your finger on. Sure, you know when you've seen or heard it, or have *been* persuaded, but most people think it's like charisma: either you've got the capacity for it or you don't. Or you might argue that how much money you're asking to borrow or how much risk you're asking your "audience" to take raises the stakes for persuasiveness (or changes them). But here's what I know from winging my way through more than a couple of pitch meetings (except for the flea-repellent dog sweaters, I've pitched everything above multiple times): no matter the stakes, the inter-related qualities of a clear vision and your conviction in it will win almost anyone over.

Clear vision involves both a well-articulated big-picture goal and a breakdown of the specific steps it'll take to get there. Conviction means you have faith in your own idea, confidence in your mission. Conviction usually comes to you once you've done the hard work of honing your vision; convince yourself first and others will follow. (I suppose conviction can be faked, but like with an orgasm, you really only ever fool the fools, and who wants to be in bed—business or the real thing—with a fool?)

Now, all this probably makes sense to you in the context of business ventures or investments, right? But let me get all Oprah on you for a minute and plant this idea in your mind: developing goals and having faith in them is the *business of life.*

Being able to articulate what makes you tick and what you want out of your time on this planet (and what you don't) is, I think, the foundation ingredient in a life well lived.

In my fantasy—see the next chapter—I am now sitting in for Oprah, so here I will pause and then look at the camera meaningfully, dropping my jaw as if to say, "Yeah, I'm blown away by this concept, too!" Eventually I'll tell the audience, "Wow. Don't go anywhere. When we come back we'll talk about how to take the next step. Be right back, back in a minute . . ."

Cue commercials for Viagra, Motrin, and Gerber life insurance.

" . . . And we're back! We're talking today about the profound idea that setting goals and developing confi-

dence in them is the key to life. Have I persuaded you to give this a try? Are you totally chomping at the bit to get started? Good! Let's take this back down to earth and get real."

(Okay, I'll stop with the guest-hosting-on-*Oprah* fantasy because it's clearly working only for me and is probably starting to annoy you. But I can't help sharing that even that little departure into my dream life has left me feeling refreshed and energized and ready to share more.)

I recommend three strategies for this life work:

The Twenty-Words-or-Less Mission Statement

This is pretty much what you think it is. It's a you-haiku. It's how you see yourself in a description that would fit on a business card. If you were trying to launch a brand, this would be your slogan. If you were trying to describe yourself at a job interview, this would be the convincing (but not cheesy) summary of your skills and drive. This twenty-words-or-less mission statement will launch the business or life of your dreams. But it's also the hardest twenty words you're ever going to have to write. And rewrite, and rewrite.

Because it often only comes to you after you've filled several garbage cans with crumpled-up sketches of the idea/event/feeling you are trying to sell (or sell to yourself).

The mistake most people make here is to try to pack too much information into what is supposed to be a very simple message. Keep at it and keep testing how genuine it sounds when you say it out loud. Too bullshitty and it'll never play. Strive to use adjectives that are colorful but not over the top (and definitely don't use big words!). Stay the hell away from office-speak like "synergy" and "win-win."

The Two-Minute Elevator Pitch

You've just stepped onto an elevator and find yourself alone with the CEO of your company, the producer you really want to work with, or the person who could make the decision to fund the nail salon of your dreams (or, if you are a deeply good soul, the person who is in charge of picking the director of that orphanage in Haiti you've been dying to work in). You have two minutes to state your case with enough detail that you will intrigue and impress but not so much that the other person doesn't want to hear or see more. When the elevator reaches the ground floor, you're shit out of time and luck. Be succinct, but be memorable. Don't step in too close—the last thing you want is for your "audience" to be pinned to the wall and desperate to get away from your enthusiasm.

Your Own Private TED Talk

If someone gave you a microphone and a stage and said, "Go ahead, talk about your hot, hot self for twenty minutes," what would you tell your audience? Because that's really what TED talks do, right? The TED folks invite people from all walks of life to come and tell the paying audience why they or their thoughts or their research or their humor is *special*. Plus, I hear they coach you and give you guidelines on making your presentation of your specialness even more special. Twenty fabulously long minutes to blow your wad *and* the assistance of someone whose job it is to help you not make a fool of yourself or bore your audience? I've got to get me some of that! Of course, no one can really coach you out of being a pompous jackass or a self-satisfied prick.

Everyone has a favorite TED talk (or a new favorite every week), and I'll admit that I've become a fan of a number of them, too. The one from several years ago by that neuroscientist who narrates the experience of having a stroke was pretty amazing. This was a major stroke (she couldn't walk or talk for many years afterward), but she knew enough about how the brain works to be aware of what was happening to her, even as she was slowly losing function. Her TED talk replays her thought process. I'm guessing she persuaded every last person in the room (not to mention countless online viewers since) that she was reliving the stroke for the first time on that stage. She was not only passionate but believable. She was herself, and not overly studied or practiced. Her story was structured (she was in command even when she was acting out how it felt to be out of control), but it seemed like she was kind of, well, improvising. My hero. We should all be that relaxed and confident and interesting after the worst thing in the world has happened to us. Practice makes perfect!

Dream It to Achieve It, Baby!

C all it visualization or call it fantasy—all I know is that being able to dream about what you want in life is a great way to begin to make it happen. Remember the complicated brain blah-blah I mentioned I'd read about in *Psychology Today* at my gyno? Well, that applies here, too— apparently if you can visualize, fantasize, or dream it in detail, you pave some kind of neurological access to the experience again.

Athletes know this, too—they visualize running the race, hitting the ball, sinking the basket, or making the putt, and then when they go to do the thing in real life, sometimes the memory of doing it successfully kicks in and twitches their muscles or tweaks their aim and they pass an opponent, hit the home run, dunk the ball, or win the tournament.

Sounds to me like it can't hurt to daydream! Which is such good news, because I just love it when something I already do anyway is proven not only to *not* be a waste of time but even to be beneficial. Here's hoping science will soon prove the usefulness of my nail biting.

I think that every woman needs to have a handful of excellent daydreams in her mental file cabinet. Three to five should do it, and on a range of topics, so that you can pull them out and escape to a happy place during long car or plane rides, boring theater productions, tedious dates, bad sex, or lectures from your boss.

One daydream/fantasy should feature you in your dream job (see the me-subbing-for-Oprah fantasy in the last chapter). Picture the scenario in superdetail. Ask yourself:

Where would you work?
Me: On Oprah's old show; I'd be her stand-in and sometime co-host. I wouldn't have to be at the studio *every* day, but she'd trust me with the trickiest topics and interviews.

How would you get there?
Me: Limo, natch!

What would your office look like?
Me: Attached private bath (see my sex fantasy on

page 150, and my feelings about stylish modern plumbing, page 169).

What would you wear to work?
Me: Whatever I want. I'd have a wardrobe budget.

How would you treat your employees?
Me: We'd all totally love each other, have the utmost respect for each other, and know the unique and perfect gift for each other at Christmas.

(Though it will be tempting to also imagine if your parents would be proud of you in this new, dreamy work role, resist the urge to go there. There is no room for mommy or daddy issues at this party!)

Another daydream should feature you standing up for yourself. The authority you tell to stick it could be your childhood nemesis, your boss, or the dentist whose lectures about flossing you're really getting tired of. This fantasy is fun—you might find that you can get really carried away in it. You can adjust the script every time, but there's something about having the plot sorted out in advance that I just know will help you someday live the same story line. Escape regularly into this happy scene and you may start to become the ballsy and confident woman you see in it.

Last but most important, one or more should definitely be about crazy-hot sex with whoever makes you wet just thinking about him. *People*'s "Sexiest Man of the Year" is an obvious place to start, but conjure up whoever does it for you and slow the scene down so you can picture every single touch, stroke, moan, and bark.

If you're happily married or in a committed relationship, I assure you that having fantasy sex with someone other than your partner is not cheating. And I assure you that he does it, too. No one needs to know; you don't need to confess it to him (unless of course you want to do a role-play thing with costumes later).

One warning: done right, this fantasy will leave you with the urge to go finish things off in private, so try to indulge in it when you have a lockable bathroom and/or your vibrator nearby.

The Single-Mom Balancing Act

After you've been married awhile you think your single friends have it made. *You* get home from work and have to do the lion's share of the meal planning, dish scrubbing, and laundry folding. You can't seem to find any of that work-life balance everyone is talking about. And you have to brush your hair and teeth *every single day* to be a semi-presentable spouse.

Meanwhile, you're sure that the singles are eating and laughing in fabulous restaurants with a new interesting man every week. When they choose to stay in, at least they only have to deal with their own mess. Any balancing act they have to do is made so much easier by not having to factor someone else into the equation. You remember it fondly (and inaccurately).

Of course, when you've been single longer than you'd like, you start to want the "guaranteed" stability of marriage. No more having to audition for strangers, no more having to hold your farts back in bed. Someone to share the balancing act with. You want a 50/50 partnership and the meaningful, mutually supportive conversations that your married friends are surely having in the calm of their clean, organized homes *every single night.*

The grass is always greener.

In some circles, being a single mom is some kind of evil syndrome, a status to be avoided at all costs—even the costs of staying in a bad marriage. But I get the feeling that some of my married mom friends *envy* my single motherhood. Do they really think my lack of a husband gives me loads of extra time for Evan or for myself (which is the order of priorities for moms everywhere, no matter what the airlines tell us about tending to our own oxygen mask first)? Ha! Look up any of the following terms in the dictionary and I'll bet there's a picture of a single mom in the margin: "winging it," "improvising," "juggling balls," "dropping balls," "hanging on by a thread."

Obviously, some people (my married mom friends among them) fantasize about having a quiet, well-behaved family unit. But I grew up in a house full of chirpy girls: me and three sisters. No dinner was ever without chatter unless Dad just wasn't having it and ordered us all to shut up. In which case one of us would inevitably shoot milk out a nostril and onto the roast while trying to suppress a giggle. There was no keeping the McCarthy girls quiet for long. Maybe my memory has glamorized the big family meal. And in the same way, my married mom friends have probably glamorized the mother-child twosome.

One friend told me she imagines me and Evan sitting in our sweats, eating out of takeout containers, me with no makeup on, no bra, and no worries, him never whining or talking back, always content to be with me. She imagines us laughing together at movies we have enthusiastically agreed to watch together. *Shrek, Cars,* or *The Incredibles* now, and maybe in a few years he'll want to see more grown-up romantic comedies (because those kids' movies are all romantic comedies at heart, did you notice that?) and laugh, roll his eyes, or tear up in all the right places. A mother, a child, no dishes, a movie, synchronized giggling: this is her idea of a heavenly evening.

Whatever that says about her married life, that's my idea of a good night, too. But it's not a frequent scene around my house. And neither is the scene from my own childhood—Evan's not going to have any siblings!

It's true that husbands do tend to take up a lot of time and energy when you're having trouble getting along with them, they do generate a lot of dishes, and they don't always want to watch our favorite shows. But not having one hasn't exactly turned every night into a cozy popcorn-and-a-movie sleepover for me and Evan.

I'll give my friend the takeout in her imagined scene. That's pretty accurate. In my fridge right now: almond milk, capers, and five leftover tater tots. Any ideas for how to whip that nasty combination into a meal? Me neither. That's why I have several delivery places on speed dial. But even when the food has arrived, or while we're waiting for it, Evan's usually got homework, which can quickly put a cloud over the house, or he'd rather be at a friend's house, or he wants to watch the dreaded *SpongeBob* or a show with lots of car wrecks—the kind I really can't stand.

And I've always got work I have to do at home, which can make me cranky. Phone calls to return, emails to write, and Internet surfing to do (which I know I should be doing less of; didn't you see my acknowledgment of my addiction on page 55?). And that's a recipe for a certain kind of disaster right there: the two of us just sort of staring at our plates, keeping our busy thoughts in our own busy little heads, while lukewarm gluten-free nuggets congeal in their own juices or lame salad wilts in its Styrofoam.

Turning on the TV doesn't solve anything (and I

know, I know, you shouldn't eat in front of the TV, but come on, you've never done it?) because when that commercial for the large, smiling "normal" family— two parents, at least two kids, and Grandma along for the ride—eating that heart-clogging Bloomin' Onion at Outback comes on, I'm likely to get kind of jealous of all that boisterous noise and big-family fun (memories of my own childhood again, I guess).

There are other situations where being the single mom can make a girl feel bad for herself. I'm not too proud to admit that at the park I've jealously watched couples picnicking with their kids from where I'm stuck in the curve on the burning-hot aluminum kiddy slide. Those curves are not made for mom asses. When Evan and I are snackless and starving (hey, I can't think of everything!), the foresight they had to load plastic snap-top tubs to the gills with neatly julienned veggies and pan-fried chicken parts says happiness to me. The only comfort I take in watching those scenes of family "bliss" is knowing that couples who spend that much time on food preparation definitely don't make much time for sex.

Neighborhood functions can also be a test of my mettle. I was recently asked to bring a dessert to a potluck, but of course my day was from hell and I'd forgotten to get anything from the bakery before it closed.

Making something was never in the cards. Evan and I only had time to stop at the package store on the way, so I dashed in and bought three bags of Chips Ahoy and a bottle of vodka. What? I brought something, didn't I? The kids seemed psyched about the cookies (kids are much less picky than we give them credit for sometimes), and the beefy father of six who grabbed the vodka and hightailed it to the bathroom to top off his fruit punch was clearly appreciative. I'm pretty sure I got the stink eye from most of the other parents, though. And in that moment, in addition to feeling a tad sorry for myself, I felt bad for poor Evan: stuck with the single, working, odd mom out, the lady who doesn't cook that often and apparently doesn't give a shit.

Then I remember there's a dad drinking my vodka in the bathroom to escape the chaos of his life. And I remember that the parents at the park seemed more concerned with disinfecting the slide than going down it. And I think of all those really peaceful, quiet, and special meals that Evan and I *have* had in front of *Shrek* and *Cars* and *The Incredibles*. And I remember lots of evenings where being cozied up next to him in a restaurant booth has been better than any date I've ever been on. (Turns out we aren't fans of the Bloomin' Onion after all, though.) Of course, sometimes the conversation isn't all that electrifying and you find yourself thinking about a romantic table for two instead. Those combo tic-tac-toe/menu placemats really do come in handy. But when we're just together, when we're talking and listening to each other, it's *way* better than the supposed comfort of a married conversation at home.

When I'm starting to long for the grass *over there*—the well-watered, nicely cut, and bright green stuff that those picnickers are sitting on, for instance—I only have to remind myself of all the things Evan and I do have and share and I am cheered right up. We have our own well-honed special thing. We really enjoy each other's company. It's during quiet and even noncommunicative meals that we learn to just be together. We get to be alone in our own little bubble. We have our own private jokes; we can crack each other up. If he happens to be drinking milk, he has been known to shoot it out his nostril—a beautiful thing to see. We are not "normal" or "conventional" in the way advertisers would have you believe is ideal, but we are *us*.

Balance is so overrated. Imbalance challenges you but can bring out your best. (An aside: did you know that most women have boobs that are slightly different sizes? That's Mother Nature acknowledging right there that balance isn't all it's cracked up to be. Yes—I really read that somewhere. Maybe not in *Psychology Today*, but probably in an old *Cosmo* I picked up while waiting in the doctor's office. Not that I told my plastic surgeon to go for imbalanced implants, though.)

We all know that parenting can be challenging, whether you're single or partnered up. And being the sole carpooler, discipliner, Band-Aid applier, nightmare calmer, and chef in your household gets old, even if it's nice to never have your authority challenged by your spouse. I know I'll get enough of that when Evan hits adolescence (and it'd only be karmic justice if he gives it to me as bad as I dished it out to my parents).

But here's what I urge: stop making it harder by beating yourself up for not being the one who can manage those massive casseroles at the potluck. Stop jonesing for some imagined perfection. This is not a scenario you can dream to achieve; it's not one you should put on your fantasy playlist (see page 148 for better ideas). Remember that just by providing a space to be with your kids, you are feeding them. You're nourishing their souls with your presence, their hearts with your understanding, and their bellies with whatever the hell you can cook up.

Remember the word "mom" in the phrase "single mom," okay? It doesn't matter how hitched you are; you are some little person's universe. Me, I give *way more* than a shit, and Evan knows it. I give great piles of it.

Giving the Bird

MASTERING THE ART OF THE FAMILY HOLIDAY MEAL

Step 1: Put turkey in the oven the day before the gathering. See Grandma's recipe below.

Step 2: Refill your Xanax prescription.

Step 3: Be strategic about the seating chart—make sure that *you* are not next to Aunt Becky. Let your husband or boyfriend do the honors.

Step 4: Pop a Xanax before your guests arrive.

Step 5: Retain easy and subtle access to the booze.

Step 6: Let someone else do the dishes.

I mentioned earlier that I have great memories of McCarthy family meals—the noise, the giggles, the camaraderie. When it comes to holiday meals, however, I have to revise the imagery a little for you.

My father has nine siblings. They all had four or five or six kids each. In other words, the McCarthy clan is enormous. When I was growing up, no one had much money, so holiday meals with his side of the family had the feel of a soup kitchen—sixty or more people shuffling in line toward a buffet of too little food.

I have vivid memories of being kissed by aunts with giant cold sores. I remember the nightmare of the "kids' table" and the cousins who could fart on command—and also when you commanded them not to.

We kids were basically left to fend for ourselves. One year, my cousins dared me to plug in the iron and press my hand on it to test how hot it could get. It's a wonder to me now that I have continued to choose the "dare" option in life, but I guess anything is a cakewalk after second-degree burns on your hands.

In my memory, Grandma McCarthy is always sitting (after pushing out ten kids, I don't blame her one bit) and some drunk is always singing an Irish tune. Someone else is often screaming at the drunk to shut up. Looking back, I'm grateful I wasn't tortured by being dry humped in a closet by a first cousin. Second or third cousin, maybe, but not a first.

As unappetizing as any of this may seem to an out-

sider, I have to admit that to me these are very soothing memories. My family is imperfect, but it's mine,
you know? From talking with friends, I'm aware that
this is a pretty universal weirdness, so maybe you feel
the same way. Everyone's brand of family insanity is
sacred and we are all a little biased toward our family
skeletons.

Which makes it hard, as we grow older and pair up,
to create new family traditions or to adapt to your
spouse's (or anyone else's) ideal of the family holiday
meal. Add in-laws or, worse, divorce to this mix and
the importance of your own traditions ratchets up even
more. Not to mention that your children become like
the wishbone you fought over when you were a kid.

I'm not proud to say that when I was married I had
trouble adapting to the blended-family holiday. I may
not have liked Grandma's bird, but I loved my mom's
recipe for stuffing and had been trained for years on
how to make it exactly like hers. When my mother-in-
law brought *her* traditional stuffing to the party, I got
irrationally uppity. I didn't like the way she imposed
her past onto my present. I'm a Scorpio, so the revenge
I took came naturally: I snuck into the kitchen and
oversalted her dish. I took it to a criminal level. People
were thirsty for days and no one but me knew why.
Now they do!

Now that I'm more "mature" and evolved (I can admit to what I did, after all), I've come to realize what only our loved ones can teach us. You don't see your own assets or your own faults in any kind of perspective until you've seen them operating in a relative. (And good or bad, you can't quite see your spouse clearly until you see him reflected in one of his blood relatives across the dining room table. Whether or not he sees himself as well is anyone's guess.)

Do you think you are an amazingly funny storyteller? Well, when you see Uncle Harold holding court, you might be humbled by *his* ability, and it's a good thing to be a little humbled.

Are you always right? Inevitably you're going to sit next to someone who has the same righteous streak, so right back atcha.

Is your cousin acting like a control freak? It probably bothers you because you could be described the same way.

I can now see that if I have a problem with anyone at my Thanksgiving dinner, it's a blessing. Your annoying relatives give you a glimpse of what annoys others about you. Identifying what you have to work on and being given the chance to do it with people who have to love you anyway is something to be truly thankful for!

Thank you, Aunt Becky, for showing me what it means to be a real asshole.

GRANDMA'S RECIPE
FOR THANKSGIVING SUCCESS

Ingredients:

1 20-pound turkey to feed 70 hungry guests

Giblets in their plastic bag

1 stick butter

Directions:

Leave all giblets in plastic and keep inside the bird.

Do not rub the butter on the bird. Leave dry.

Keep the stick of butter in its wrapper and shove inside the bird cavity.

Set oven to 200 degrees and cook the bird low and slow for 24 hours. Do not baste.

When bird ignites, it is *almost* done.

Serve with cold mashed potatoes and Jell-O shots.

Expect no leftovers.

Happy Thanksgiving!

Pep Talk

> ## RECIPE FOR SUCCESS
> ■ ■ ■ ■ ■ ■ ■ ■ ■ ■ ■ ■ ■ ■ ■ ■ ■ ■ ■
>
> **Ingredients:**
>
> *1 brand-new day*
>
> *1 brand-new attitude*
>
> *1 brand-new you*
>
> *1 brand-new bathing suit*

I've said earlier that some fantasizing is healthy and primes your mind for success. (And don't forget about the way it also primes your crotch muscles to be able to have that orgasm when what he's doing down there isn't really working.) But when we don't want to do the hard work that goes along with getting the dream job or finding the dream man or creating the dream life—when we'd really like those opportunities to knock on the door with the Chinese takeout or come wrapped in a blue Tiffany box and white satin bow, thank you

very much—we are in trouble. Warning: When you catch yourself feeling underappreciated, take notice. Feeling underappreciated is just a psychological cover for feeling sorry for yourself. Were you not paying attention at all during my "Reverse Psychology" lecture? Let me spell it out one more time:

Your Dream + Taking Steps to Make Good Things Happen = Success

Your Dream + Entitlement = Big Fat Fucking Failure (plus, no one will really like you)

If I had a dollar for every time I felt sorry for myself because something wasn't going my way, I'd be richer than Donald Trump. (I already have better boobs than him, but richer would be nice, too. You thought I was going to go with better hair, didn't you? Too easy a target.) What an easy way to make money that would be!

I've tried every feeling-sorry-for-myself approach in the book. I've tried keeping my self-pity to myself, and I've also complained loudly to my friends and loved ones. I've sat around on my lazy ass quietly whining, moping, and binge-eating myself into my fat pants. I've done it all loudly as well. I've vowed to be patient and think happy thoughts and wait my turn, and I've

also called my manager and agent begging, pleading, and crying about wanting better things to float my way.

And, of course, none of these strategies changed a damn thing. Know what did? I think it was something in the hoping-something-would-float-my-way imagery that clicked for me. This single-sentence realization finally did the trick: *If your ship doesn't come in, swim out to it!*

In other words, if the life you want doesn't magically come to you (which it rarely does, though see Paris Hilton and Kim Kardashian references, page 134), you have to go out and get it. Then live the shit out of the opportunities you create for yourself!

When the float-vs.-swim-out-to-your-ship idea first dawned on me, I couldn't wait to start making a list. There's nothing like a list to focus your energy, and it feels so great when you accomplish something and can cross it off the list.

At the top of the page I wrote "On My Ship" and then listed all the things I wished for and wanted. I'm talking everything: a new boyfriend, a new career, more time for Evan, a new stove, smaller pants, copper plumbing, landscaping in my yard, et cetera. No matter how trivial it was, if I wanted it, I put it on my list.

Then I created a sub-list—the ship that had the things I couldn't buy (when I had the money), the less tangible, less easily accomplished goals that I *really* wanted to try for. These were the things that would better my life, my spirit, and my well-being (the stove, copper plumbing, and the services of a gardener were obviously not on it). This was the ship I made it a priority to swim for first. Then, one by one, I found a way to go after these big wants.

Truth: Instead of waiting for someone to ask me to write my first book, I wrote one. Then I went to publishers and searched for the one whose team shared my vision of becoming a successful author.

Truth: When no one would cast me in a TV show, I wrote myself into my own story concepts and scripts, and then went to every studio and network with a smile on my face and pitched the crap out of my shows.

Truth: During a particularly dry dating spell—I just couldn't find a man worth bonking—I asked people around me who had very high personal standards to set me up with men they thought would be good for me.

Now, not all of my books have sold gazillions, not all of my TV show ideas saw the light of day or lasted long when they did, not every blind date turned into a boyfriend or even a roll in the hay . . . *but that wasn't the point of making the effort!*

Are you following this pep talk at all? The point was, I swam out to my ship! I went after the things I wanted in my life instead of going the easier (and dicey) route of sitting back and waiting. Instead of nursing the wounds of self-pity, I put myself out there, put my ass on the line, and let myself be vulnerable to failure. Because when you're vulnerable to failure you're also vulnerable to success. I'm not saying it's easy, but it's worth it. Honest to God, swear on my awesome life: self-doubt, inaction, and indecision kill more dreams than failure ever could. I now know that I'm too smart for doubt, inaction, and indecision even on my blondest day.

OTHER HALFTIME LOCKER ROOM ENCOURAGEMENT

The past is behind you, so there's no reason to keep beating yourself up over what you didn't do right.

The present is now. You're either living all over it or it's living all over you—that's your choice.

The future is a big block of clay waiting for you to mold it into something spectacular.

You don't need anyone's permission to seek happiness. Life is not one big traffic light at which you have to wait your turn. See the green light and floor it.

Changing your ways may be difficult at first and it's hard to gain momentum, but once you get your stroke down, you'll be swimming full steam out to your own ship.

It feels better living in the skin of someone who braves the ocean tides to swim to her destiny than living in the skin of someone braving the sofa in her fat pants feeling sorry for herself.

My Resolution to Go Slow

One of my best characteristics is that I'm spontaneous—I can shift gears, scrap plans, and get on board with your new idea quickly. I'm more of a "Yes, let's give that a whirl" person than a skeptical, conservative "Let's wait and see" type. Spontaneity works for me. Being cautious and suspicious doesn't feel like a very pleasant way to go through life, and slamming on the brakes just leaves me carsick.

Another thing I like about myself is that I don't judge. I am more than willing to talk to and hang with seeming weirdos, the ones most people don't even give a second look. The payoff is that I click with the most surprising and unlikely people. It's an awesome feeling to mesh with another soul, especially when that other soul didn't look all that promising to others. Whether that person is a friend or a lover, it's so energizing to hum along at the same frequency. Two peas in a pod and all that. The new relationship is like a drug, and being with the other person is your fix.

Okay, before you freak out, I do see that if you need a fix, you're a junkie, and most junkies aren't known for their good decision-making skills. Yes, I'll admit that nine times out of ten, all that intimacy and soul connection dissipates when you drop the whole person-on-a-pedestal thing (or put your damn glasses on and see the person in better focus in the morning). And it's true that when you're willing to click with people as freely as I am, you sometimes make a house key for people who should probably just be passing acquaintances. (That's not a metaphor; I make a lot of house keys and have probably single-handedly kept the local locksmith in business.)

Yes, through some really spectacularly bad decisions and character assessments, I've come to realize that there's a fine line between what's positive about being spontaneous and what's dangerous about being impulsive, between the benefits of not judging and the idiocy of not using your head. I can admit that I cross these lines all the fucking time.

If I like your idea, I too often don't ask the right follow-up questions. Instead I jump in with both feet without really considering your true agenda or the consequences. This is as true about getting a dramatic new haircut as it is about making a business deal. Hair grows back. But money, once it's been flushed down the toilet of an ill-considered venture . . . not so much.

Here's one example of a pool into which I should have dipped my pinky toe instead of cannonballing. I once met a lady while standing in line at a pharmacy. We had the same shampoo in our baskets, so we got to talking. We quickly discovered that we had compatible astrological signs, so before we'd even reached the checkout, we were discussing plans to start an online horoscope company together. We had exchanged contact info before we made it to the parking lot, and let's just say I went further down that particular toilet pipe than I should have.

Another time I met a woman at my boot camp fitness class who seemed really motivated and knowledgeable. She mentioned she was looking for work and a place to stay, so I offered her a job as a live-in personal trainer and cleaned out my guest room for her (yes, of course she got a key to my house). After the initial burst of workout energy between us wore off (which took a couple of days), she mostly read *Us Weekly* and left my couch full of potato chip crumbs. My treadmill became a handy drying rack for her hand-washables for six months. I suppose all I really lost was a little muscle tone and a guest room. On the upside, her *Us Weekly* subscription still comes to my house.

Then there was the assistant hairdresser on location during filming . . . he kept my orgasms flowing during a bitterly cold snap but emptied the minibar, my per diem allowance, and my wallet. I didn't want for things to be weird, though, so I let him stay for the entire three months of production. On the upside, did I mention those orgasms? I kept warm and satisfied that winter, so that's something.

I'm told that I'm lucky that letting the wrong person too quickly into my life hasn't led to worse. I've never been stabbed (did I mention that another thing I like about myself is that I can always see the bright side of things?). But I'm guessing that my guardian angel is working overtime, and I know it's time to give her a chance to rest.

So—drumroll, please—here's what I've resolved to do this year: I'm going to look before I leap into bed, research before I invest, and take the locksmith off speed dial. There, I did that last one already. I'm on a roll.**

I see from watching Evan that it can take hours, days, or even months to master a video game. Inspired by the time and energy he puts into advancing through each level, I have an idea to devise a point system for moving a semi-stranger up the ladder of my affections. Everyone starts as a potential friend (hey, I can't start judging now; everyone has potential!) but has to prove trustworthiness in order to become a friend, good friend, great friend, BFF, lover, or profound love of my life. I'm not clear yet on what will qualify as trustworthiness (because my measurement of that quality hasn't exactly been accurate in the past; page 175), but I'm working on that. All I do know is that even if it means handcuffing myself to the radiator until the impulse to make keys passes, it will now take more than a similar taste in booze, shoes, or shampoo, more than a great eye for fabric, and more than a fabulous ass or abs for someone to make it into the inner circle of my heart, my home, or my vagina.

* I made this resolution at 11:54 p.m. on December 31, 2013. I was in New York City's Times Square, helping Ryan Seacrest do the countdown honors. I was tired out from a three-day battle with the flu. I had a temperature of 103 degrees. I believe this makes me less responsible for the resolution than I would have been in my right mind.

** At this writing I have still managed to avoid making any new keys. But ask me if that's true by the time this book is in stores.

A Manopausal Road Map

We women get some conflicting messages from the media and our culture. On one hand, we are sold products and fashions that will help us, we're told, to look and feel younger. But then just as often we are told that really evolved souls surrender gracefully to age and let Mother Nature do her thing. They don't fight the way their boobs, bellies, body hair, and brains are changing.

I take a middle road. I'm not fool enough to think that I can hang on to the body I had when I was twenty years old. On the other hand, I'm not cool with rogue body hair—there really is no use for hair on a woman's chinny-chin-chin.

But let's stop analyzing the female experience for a minute here and examine how men are getting similarly confusing messaging. On one hand, our popular male role models seem to get wiser and sexier as they get older and grayer, but on the other, we make them question their own virility with all those ads for boner meds and testosterone replacement therapy. Since most men don't really talk to each other about these things, I believe they need some straight talk about what to expect as they get older, and I'm just the girl for the job. Let's get started.

LETTER TO THE MAN
GOING THROUGH MANOPAUSE

Dear Mr. Manopause:

In addition to being a son, a brother, and a friend, you may now also be a father, an uncle, or perhaps even a grandfather (depending on how young you were when you started sowing your big bad seed in the first place). Don't let anyone tell you otherwise: this adding-of-roles stage of your life is a time to celebrate. It's not a time for anxiety or fear. But I know that no one really tells you what to expect or how to cope with your changing body and priorities. So see below. Some of the bullet points are must-dos, while others are milestones to watch for. All of them should put your mind at ease about the passage into the prime of life.

• *Even though it was never an option when you were in the army, "surrender" is not a dirty word.*

Now that you are maturing, it's something you need to get used to. You will have to surrender your VIP pass to the gentlemen's club or at least let it expire. On the flip side, you really should stop surrendering your credit card to the makers of Penis Power and the surprisingly chinless plastic surgeon who wants to share the 411 on injectables.

- *You will likely lose your hair. Even if you don't lose your hair, what little you have will lose its color. Don't fight this change with dye. A silver fox can be smoking hot. A guy who turns the pillow brown if he sweats in his sleep never is.*

- *If you're concerned about your sex drive, you don't need to be. Any woman will tell you that thinking about it is half the battle. (It's when it never crosses your mind that you might be done . . . but if it never crosses your mind, you won't be worrying about it.)*

- *True midlife is when most men stop thinking so much about how to attract the ladies and start focusing more on how to keep the ladies. In other words, if you haven't figured out where her clitoris is yet, you're not quite yet in your prime. Keep working at it.*

- *Your balls will start to get longer and the day will*

come when you realize free-ballin' has to be a thing of your past. This shouldn't trouble you. Wearing underwear is preferable to ball chafe around your knees.

- *You'll be unable to resist buying box sets of Steely Dan and Rush, and you'll find yourself wondering out loud (to other prime-timers) why the hell you didn't keep all your vinyl. Let it go—you sold it at a yard sale and there's no going back.*

- *You may also find yourself reminiscing about the drugs you took when you first saw Steely Dan or Rush live. You and your manopausal brothers will talk fondly of Thai sticks and lids and seeds and stems, LSD, and that time you cured a ten-year-old heartbreak with just one handful of 'shrooms. Nothing wrong with going down memory lane, but consult your physician if you have the urge to relive any of those days for real.*

- *You may experience the urge to purchase a bright yellow sports car. As long as the urge doesn't also include wanting to drive around picking up underage girls, caving in to the purchase of a statement vehicle is nothing to be ashamed of. Still, since the chances are good that you will become embarrassed by it within a couple of years, you should consider leasing instead of buying.*

- *Some of you will continue to skateboard. Others of you will take surfing lessons. Some of you will spend lots of time perfecting your golf swing. Others of you will get it into your head that you want to run a marathon. Whatever floats your boat. Nothing wrong with exercise.*

- *Please understand once and for all that there is no such thing as the diet of a "real man." If you love steak and scotch and cigars, enjoy them (though you'll last longer in bed and on this earth if you lay off all those heart-cloggers a little). If you like quiche and quinoa and kale, knock yourself out (but keep in mind that incessant talk about health food and bowel movements is a total turn-off).*

- *Last one, so pay close attention: even if you're with a whole new cast of characters in this Act II of your life, you're going to need to make amends and make peace with the people who were on-stage with you for Act I. I'm talking about first wives, Mister, so Make It Right.*

Four Things Every Girl
Should Have in Her Purse

Wallet, keys, lipstick? Obviously. Here is your advanced packing list:

1. Earbuds. Clearly, these come in handy when you want to listen to your favorite tunes or watch back episodes of your favorite sitcom on your iPad without bothering the lady next to you on the train. But they are also an incredibly diplomatic decoy: tuck the plug inside your purse and pretend you're listening to music even if you're not. I find this is a much nicer and more effective way to communicate "I'm not interested in talking to you" than your middle finger. The middle finger tends not to shut people up. Go figure.

2. Individually wrapped hard candies. Throw the candy at random, untethered children or even random, untethered men who approach you. They

always scatter like pigeons chasing feed and you can make your getaway.

3. Chopsticks. Chopsticks don't take up much room at all, but they have several important uses. If you're coordinated enough to feed yourself with them, you're already ahead of the game. But I tend to use chopsticks either to put my hair up (instructions: twist your hair into a bun and stab the chopsticks through it in a crisscross) or as an amazingly effective weapon now that Mace has been outlawed in some states. Especially if those earbuds aren't doing the trick . . .

4. Emergency feminine protection products. As many as you can jam into an opaque bag that will fit inside your purse while still leaving just enough room for your wallet, keys, lipstick, earbuds, candy, and chopsticks. See "The Red Scare," page 59, if you don't have a firm handle on why this is so important.

Pooper Scooping

To borrow from the 1960s Virginia Slims cigarette commercial, I've come a long way, baby!

Of course, that slogan was somehow meant to appeal to "liberated" working women, the idea being that black lungs and yellowed fingertips were no longer the kind of reward for hard work that only men should enjoy.

Even though I've had trouble kicking my own nicotine habit, we can all laugh at the ridiculousness of that ad now. Nothing says confidence and sex appeal like having to drag around an oxygen tank, right?

But there was a time when no one did laugh at it. We bought into the idea hook, line, and sinker, just like we've done with lots of other subliminal and not-so-subliminal messages sold to us over the years. That's the nature of advertising and marketing, and I'm not here to judge the results, okay? That's what lawsuits and the Surgeon General are for.

But to be corny for a minute, the life cycle of that old ad campaign—both what it stood for and the punch line it later became—are not so far from the cycle of life itself. Don't we all just keep naively looking for direction in the wrong places? Don't we buy into the latest trends and expert opinions only to wake up at some point to the realization that we were fucking idiots back then? Don't you sometimes look at photos of your younger self and wish you could give the person in that snapshot a massive head slap? You know you do. We all occasionally wish for a time machine that could give us a chance to warn ourselves about the pain, disappointment, and rude awakenings to come.

But short of inventing that time machine, the kindest thing you can do for yourself is to not spend time on regret. Instead, choose to smile at your naïveté. Have the 2014 version of yourself let the 1990 version of yourself go. Don't head-slap that girl in the photos; instead, whisper to her that you know she was doing the best she could with what she had to work with. Through the healing power of YouTube, I am constantly amused by the naïveté of some of the things that've come out of my mouth; I am constantly amused by my choice in acting jobs, even if very few other people are.

More than anything, *that's* the way in which I've come a long way. I've given up regretting things because it's so fucking futile to shoulda, coulda, woulda yourself all day. Even painful things like job disappointment and relationship rejection—things that chewed me up to a point I could barely stand at the time—have eventually spit me out in a good place. My mistakes and my pain and my baggage have made me the successful, *happy* person that I am today.

Now, I'm not only saying that when life gives you lemons, make lemonade. And I'm not only saying that what doesn't kill you makes you stronger. Instead, I'll put it in a way no Hallmark card would dare: *the way to wisdom is through the shit.*

In your lifetime you will encounter small piles like the ones the lady with the poodle refuses to pick up on your block, and massive steaming piles of it, like the bucketloads the clowns have to clean up as they run behind the elephants at the circus. Some people try to step around it every time, but me, I embrace even the nastiest of it in some small way. Sometimes I step in it, and sometimes I pick it up and throw it aside. Sometimes I even add a few ingredients, stir it up, and voilà—I've transformed it into something useful, like (metaphorically speaking) a spa mud mask.

However you choose to deal with the shit in the path of your life, don't take it personally. After all, neither the dog nor the elephant is thinking about you when it drops a wet load near your shoe. It's just life.

Found on the Cutting Room Floor: Alternative Titles for This Book

Winging It: The Screwball Method to My Madness

Repeatedly Tarred and Feathered: Confessions of an Out-spoken Midwesterner

Shortcuts and Big Butts: Musings on the Kardashian Rise to Fame

From Playmates to Playdates: A Memoir

Mastering the Art of the Artful Fuck-Up

31,437 Words of Advice . . . and Other Reasons to Drink

Ball Dropping: A Single Mother's Life

You've Come a Long Way, Baby: My Life in Commercial Slogans

*Slurping Soup and Busting Nuts: My Get-Ahead Plan for
Conquering Hollywood*

Truth or Dare: The Jenny McCarthy Story

Acknowledgments

I couldn't have done this book without you, kids (okay, maybe I could have but it would have been a lot harder). Thanks to:

My dedicated agent, Jennifer Rudolph Walsh.

The most talented editor in publishing, Marnie Cochran.

My creative research team, Amirra Ruotola Behrendt, Paula Killen, and Brett Paesel.

My mother. Sorry I stole your recipes for this book. I love you.

ABOUT THE AUTHOR

JENNY MCCARTHY is the author of ten books, including the *New York Times* bestsellers *Belly Laughs: The Naked Truth About Pregnancy and Childbirth; Baby Laughs: The Naked Truth About the First Year of Mommyhood; Louder than Words: A Mother's Journey in Healing Autism; Love, Lust, & Faking It: The Naked Truth About Sex, Lies, and True Romance;* and *Bad Habits: Confessions of a Recovering Catholic.* Getting her start as the host of MTV's hugely popular dating show *Singled Out,* McCarthy has had a high-profile television and film career and has been a guest on virtually every television talk show, from *The Oprah Winfrey Show, Larry King Live, The View, Ellen,* and *Late Show with David Letterman,* to *Conan, Hannity & Colmes,* and *The Howard Stern Show.* A co-host of ABC's *The View* since September 2013, she also co-hosts *Dick Clark's New Year's Rockin' Eve* with Ryan Seacrest, writes an advice column for the *Chicago Sun-Times,* and tours nationally for her *Dirty Sexy Funny* stand-up show. She lives outside of Chicago with her son, Evan.

www.jennymccarthy.com
Facebook.com/JennyMcCarthyOfficial
@JennyMcCarthy
Instagram.com/JennyAnnMcCarthy

ABOUT THE TYPE

This book was set in Garamond, a typeface originally designed by the Parisian type cutter Claude Garamond (c. 1500–61). This version of Garamond was modeled on a 1592 specimen sheet from the Egenolff-Berner foundry, which was produced from types assumed to have been brought to Frankfurt by the punch cutter Jacques Sabon (c. 1520–80).

Claude Garamond's distinguished romans and italics first appeared in *Opera Ciceronis* in 1543–44. The Garamond types are clear, open, and elegant.